MW01293915

because Paul writes about what was most important to him, his faith in Jesus Christ, and how that disciplined his entire life and career. This is an All-Star book written by a Hall-of-Famer All-Star. It isn't just a good read, it's a GREAT READ!"
– Rev. Larry and Lily Fultz, Parents of Tim Fultz

"Three things Paul and I had in common: Jesus, basketball, and Coach John Wooden. Coach Wooden and I met when I was a young boy, and I went to his camps out at Cal Lutheran. My dad played for coach Wooden and earned a full ride to UCLA 1959-62. Years later, we would reconnect and my wife, Kerri, and I would have Coach and his daughter, Nan, over for dinner with our friend Vicki, who was his assistant at UCLA. Paul's name always came up. Well, what is written in this book from Paul about Coach Wooden is all true because Coach Wooden says the same thing, only Coach Wooden would tell the story about Paul but way more earnestly. He was still pained as Westy went to USC. ('My prodigal son who went to that school on the east side') Coach always told me how that one hurt the worst. That story is in this very book that you should buy right this second! Paul's intelligent humor is all over this book.

Most of my time with Paul was over the phone on long conversations about life while I was in some jungle in Africa or a remote island in the Pacific. It always worked its way back to The Truth … Jesus. At times maddening voices in our heads but one sound in the Heart … Jesus.

It came down to the end of his life; a great life, a very beautiful life. Paul, I am haunted reading this special book. I will need it as a reminder as I have not finished 'my race.'"
– Jim Caviezel, former college basketball player, actor

FOREWORD
BY LEN MUNSIL
PRESIDENT, ARIZONA CHRISTIAN UNIVERSITY

Growing up in the Valley in the 1970s, long before the Arizona Cardinals and Diamondbacks, the Phoenix Suns were the only game in town.

As a twelve-year-old seventh grader who loved sports, I remember the Suns' run to the NBA finals in the 1975–76 season like it was yesterday. I listened to every game on the radio with legendary broadcaster Al McCoy and made sure to mark the few regular season televised games on my calendar.

The Suns were an average regular-season team, finishing just two games above .500, but they caught fire in the playoffs, eventually upsetting defending NBA champion Golden State in the Western Conference finals. Thanks to a connected friend, I was in Veterans Memorial Coliseum—the Madhouse on McDowell—to watch the Suns defeat the Warriors in Game 6 in double overtime and stay alive. No one expected them to win Game 7 in Oakland, but they did and the whole town—which was much smaller then—went crazy as the underdog Suns advanced to their first NBA Finals appearance against the Celtics, which included the classic triple overtime "loss" in Game 5 in Boston Garden. And as all of us know who lived here then, the Suns were just one bad non-call away from winning the NBA championship that season ("Blow the whistle and call the technical foul, Richie Powers!").

The Suns' two biggest stars were new to the team that year and quickly became my two favorite players—Rookie of the Year Alvan Adams, and USC star and former Celtic Paul Westphal. They were roommates, and I loved listening to Al McCoy night after night describing the amazing athletic exploits of "Westy and the Oklahoma Kid."

As a basketball-loving teenager with average-sized parents, I already knew I was never going to be a six-foot, nine-inch center like "Double A." I quickly adopted Paul Westphal as my role model. I tried to shoot like him. I worked on my fast-break spin move with a left-hand finish. A turn-around jumper with legs flying out to draw contact. I adopted his pre-free throw ritual. I had his poster on the wall of my bedroom. And I wore Number 44 on every youth league team where I could pick my number.

While Westy was dominating the NBA during the late 1970s, and the Suns were contending for a championship every year, I finished high school and was working during college as a professional sportswriter at the *Scottsdale Daily Progress*. On the dark day the Suns traded Westphal to the Seattle SuperSonics, our sports editor let me write an opinion column expressing my displeasure about the trade. While injuries undermined his time in Seattle, he became the NBA's Comeback Player of the Year with the Knicks, and as I followed every step of his NBA journey, he remained my favorite player. I was thankful he was able to finish his career with the Suns.

Years later, a mutual friend invited Tracy and me to her home to have dinner with Paul and Cindy Westphal. Finally, a chance to meet my boyhood hero!

When Paul discovered I was a Christian attorney fighting for conservative, family values, and that Tracy and I were raising our family of eight kids, he turned to me and said, "Wow, you guys are my heroes."

Having your boyhood hero call you his hero—was hard for me to fathom. It still is.

Thus began a three-decade relationship that became a deep friendship after I became President of Arizona Christian University in 2010.

I knew Paul had begun his coaching career at then-Southwestern Conservative Baptist Bible College in the mid-1980s. But at the time I didn't know the full story of that season—the story he tells in this book.

Over the next decade Paul and Cindy threw themselves into the life of the University, attending events (including basketball games), supporting scholarship programs, speaking to students and teams, and even delivering the address at ACU's Commencement ceremony. Paul and Cindy agreed to allow ACU to feature Paul's name and likeness for the "Westphal Athletic Fund"—our booster program to support ACU's NAIA athletics teams. Our ESPY-award-like season-ending athletics celebration is called "The Westphal Awards," and the culminating award—the highest award any student can receive—is for being the "Best Teammate." That was what Paul wanted the award named in his honor to stand for.

Perhaps the biggest sacrifice Paul made was to serve for six years—two consecutive three-year terms—on ACU's Board of Trustees. I say the biggest sacrifice because Paul famously hated meetings, especially ACU Board meetings. He loved the people, but he hated the meetings. Every year, with a painful, apologetic expression, he would ask me if there was anything else he could do to help the school—other than continue serving on the Board. I assured him that having him on the Board of Trustees was hugely beneficial to ACU. Paul was loved and admired, especially in Arizona, and having him on our Board gave us great credibility and helped us recruit higher profile members. His fellow Trustees loved him, and he was a strong and critical voice of support when ACU made the leap to a much larger campus in 2019. We miss him at ACU.

I had the unique experience of getting to know and become friends with someone I had idolized my entire life. We were so blessed to be included among family and friends in 2019 to watch when Paul was inducted into the Naismith Basketball Hall of Fame in Springfield, Massachusetts. Typically, the Westphals did not allow us to honor Paul—instead they held a brunch where Paul and Cindy blessed everyone in attendance by introducing us to each other and honoring each person and family by explaining our role in their amazing life.

So often you hear stories of people meeting their childhood idols and being sorely disappointed. For me, it was the exact opposite. The more I got to know Paul, the more I loved him. He was funny, competitive, generous, and kind, except when he was teasing you (especially on the golf course). He knew the best restaurants in every city. He loved discussing music and movies and books, and always had an interesting and unique take. He was one of the greatest raconteurs I've ever known—whether in a public speech, on the golf course, or over dinner—he had the ability to set up and illustrate a story, warm it up to a climactic point, and bring it to a humorous conclusion, almost always making a larger point.

And what stories! Through his fascinating life, we are brought into engaging interactions with personalities from Michael Keaton to Charles Barkley, Rush Limbaugh to John Wooden, Bill Gaither to Pete Maravich. I'm so glad that many more people will now get to experience Paul's storytelling abilities through the publication of this book.

Having interacted with a few celebrities, from presidents to professional athletes, I can say that Paul Westphal was the most down-to-earth, un-self-conscious celebrity I've ever known. He just didn't believe he was a very big deal, even though he was. It was clear that he felt like the luckiest guy on earth—just a kid who loved basketball and turned out to be pretty good at it, both as an athlete and strategically as a coach. His creativity and innovation as a player carried over into how he viewed the game as a coach. He thought the game should be fun, even when you were getting paid.

He viewed life the same way. He was thankful that God chose to bless him with such a great life—marrying his college sweetheart, Cindy, raising kids he adored, and playing and coaching a game he truly loved. He recognized life as a gift from God, and his faith was not only never shaken, but was growing year by year and demonstrated to others as he battled brain cancer. In his later speeches, even before the diagnosis, he spoke more often about the brevity of life, and was becoming more vocal in proclaiming—as he did on national television at the Hall of Fame induction ceremony—that faith in Jesus Christ is the only way to achieve true immortality.

I remain incredibly thankful to have lived out the experience of meeting and becoming friends with my boyhood hero—and discovering that he was an even better person than I could have imagined from a distance. And I'm so excited that now, through the pages of this book, many more will be able to get to know him as well.

(L-R) Dr. Tracy Munsil, Len Munsil, Pastor Larry Fultz, Cindy Westphal, and Paul Westphal at the Tim Fultz Memorial Classic basketball tournament on the campus of Arizona Christian University in 2019.

DEDICATION

Virtually every person named in this book has been special to me in a very personal way. Certainly the love shown to me by my mother Ruth Sallenbach Westphal, wife Cindy Paden Westphal, and daughter Tori Westphal Higa deserves to be honored in this dedication. But the men who have shaped my life are who I am choosing to focus on here.

Father figures mostly. But many were like sons to me. And brothers. Some, like Cotton Fitzsimmons and Howard Slusher, seemed to combine the father-and-brother relationship at various times in our lives.

I describe some great times and some bumps along the way. I have tried to smooth out the bumps, big-picture guy that I am. They do tend to smooth out in the light of eternity. But one can't tell real stories without mentioning difficulties and differences along the road to, hopefully, reconciliation. Some bumps are a distant memory. Some are hidden within these pages and seem like mountains, even now. But I have love for every person mentioned in this book, and I pray it shows.

I dedicate the stories that follow to my father Armin, brother Bill, and son Michael. With gratitude, love, and hope.

TABLE OF CONTENTS

PREFACE
TWO OPPOSITE SEASONS

After he had enjoyed retirement for a couple of years, former Knicks Coach Red Holzman was asked by the NBA to preside over an old-timers' game. This was before the League stopped this sort of nonsense due to fear of injuries and heart attacks that are inevitable when out-of-shape, old athletes try to compete in basketball.

The game was televised, and Red's team made a huge run right before the half. One of Craig Sager's predecessors had the job of asking a quick question as the teams left the court. "Red, your guys ran off twenty unanswered points to finish the half! How did you do it?"

"I'm retired now, so I can tell you what I could never admit before. How should I know? You try things. Sometimes they work, sometimes they don't."

Former Princeton Coach Pete Carril is another Hall of Fame coach whose insights always brought extra perspective to a situation. While we worked together with the Sacramento Kings, I complained to him about a troublesome player. "Coach, I don't believe he will ever change."

"I've been working with kids all my life," said Pete. "If I believed that, I would quit. I've seen people change."

The voice of wisdom had spoken.

Then he continued, "But hardly ever."

I've been involved with the highest levels of basketball for more than forty-five years, and the statements above are a good summary of what I know to be true. By recounting my experiences of coaching two opposite teams—the late 1990s era Seattle SuperSonics and the 1985–86 Southwestern Conservative Baptist Bible College Eagles (now Arizona

Christian University)—and mixing in some stories along the way, I hope to supply some insights, not only into life on the basketball court, but also in real life.

To contrast the stories of these two seasons, it is necessary to explain many of the influences and experiences that formed me and positioned me to live a life immersed in basketball. Although not an autobiography, certain biographical realities must be included to put those two seasons into their proper context. Chronology will be virtually ignored as I piece together lessons I've learned, not only about basketball, but also about music, religion, race, politics, and truth from some of the truly iconic people I've encountered. And also, lessons from people that few have heard of, like Tim Fultz, Nick Comitas, and Ken Brown—who have much to teach us.

The desire for role models in our culture is remarkable. In the early 1990s, Charles Barkley famously made a commercial that declared neither he, nor any other athlete, had a responsibility to be a role model. "It's up to parents to guide their own kids." For some reason, his remarks created an uproar. My wife, Cindy, witnessed the following exchange take place in the stands during a 1993 playoff game. A father, who was sitting with his ten-year-old son, screamed red-faced curses at Barkley.

"Besides the fact that you're rooting for the other team, why do you hate him so much?" she turned and asked.

"Because he's not a role model!" was the man's reply.

But role models do exist. Choosing a good one, that's the rub. One can learn a lot of basketball from watching NBA players, but life lessons are more likely to come from more humble places.

The Seattle SuperSonics of the late 1990s doubted there was anything they could learn from a tiny Bible college team that played together in 1986. I mean, what can any of us learn from the story of a rag-tag, fictional-sounding team from Southwestern Conservative Baptist Bible College that seemed to belong in an America that only existed in the black-and-white television shows of the 1950s?

A lot, I hoped.

Still do.

CHAPTER 1
SAME GYM, DIFFERENT SEAT

"It ain't the gold
that keeps your wheels a-turning when you're old.
It ain't the fame
that keeps a warhorse playing in the game.
It's not the end, it's the beginning,
Not the fall, it is the pinning.
So here's to 'Errol Flynning,'
That is the winning.
It ain't the gold."

— John Stewart[1]

The last time I had been in the gym on the campus of Concordia University in Irvine, California, the school was called Christ College. Now, twenty-seven years later, I was buying a ticket to watch the final game of the Golden State Athletic Conference Basketball Tournament. The winner of the game between Concordia and Arizona Christian University would receive an automatic bid to the NAIA National Championship Tournament in Kansas City. Admission was $5 for students, $10 for adults, and $8 for seniors (age sixty-two and over). I handed the kid at the table a twenty. Without hesitating, he passed me my ticket and $12 change. I had experienced my sixty-second birthday a couple of months earlier, but it still hadn't sunk in that I was eligible for senior discounts. Especially without requesting one or being asked to prove it by producing my ID. But this ticket taker had looked at me and decided I qualified. How could he know?

Christ College was the best gym in our conference in 1986. It was also the *only* gym. But it was, and still is, an outstanding small-college facility.

---

1 John Stewart, "Gold," Track #1 on *Bombs Away Dream Babies.* RSO Records, 1979.

I was the coach of the Southwestern Conservative Baptist Bible College team during the 1985–86 season. Christ College beat us by fifty-six points in this same gym that year, but I still can't remember being part of a more transcendent season.

Southwestern College is now Arizona Christian University. And like defending NAIA national champion Concordia University, the school had come a long way in the last twenty-seven years. ACU had grown, under the leadership of President Len Munsil, from a very small Bible college into a university where students could expect to obtain a wide variety of degrees at a strongly biblical, conservative university. Just try finding many of those! Additionally, it stressed an emphasis on excellence in athletics. I very much wanted to support Coach Jeff Rutter and his team by catching this game in person.

As I watched Concordia prevail 112–111 in double overtime, in a game every bit as exciting and well-played as one might expect, I couldn't help but reminisce. My mind drifted to memories of all the interesting places basketball had taken me. Playing against everyone from Wilt Chamberlain to Michael Jordan, and coaching during a time that spanned the eras of both Shaquille O'Neal and LeBron James. As a player, I'd set scoring records—been injured, traded, cut from the team, selected to All-Star teams—and also benched. As a coach, I'd often won big, and also had been fired. But it was the year I spent coaching Tim Fultz and the little team at Southwestern College—it was that special team I couldn't get out of my mind as I sat in that gym and contemplated what I have loved most about sports.

The journey.

Not the fame. Not the money. Not even the exhilaration of competition.

Success and failure are concepts that can drive a person crazy. The year I earned my biggest paycheck was one of my worst seasons. And the year I didn't make a dime was a season I wouldn't trade for ten NBA championships.

Now I'm not saying the scoreboard doesn't matter, because without the scoreboard, the beauty that competition exposes can't be seen. Without a scoreboard, all that's left is practice. What I'm saying is this: it's the respect that one gives and receives from the quest to win that lasts, not the wins or losses. It's the relationships, the shared struggles and memories.

It ain't the gold.

CHAPTER 2

GETTING FIRED

The first time I got fired was easy. My part-time job in high school was scooping ice cream at Baskin-Robbins. I was about to quit anyway. Boysenberry Sherbet, probably one of the top three flavors ever made, was about to be phased out of the Big 31, never to return as far as I knew. Once that happened, why would I stay? But the other times, getting fired would hurt. Sometimes it is unavoidable. Often, it is even a relief. It can lead to something better, and it can even be a blessing.

But it still hurts.

When I returned home after Jerry Colangelo fired me as head coach of the Phoenix Suns in 1996, the first thing I did was reach down to pat the head of our beloved little Cocker Spaniel, Barkleigh Sue. Is there any love more unconditional than the love of one's Cocker Spaniel? I doubt it, but that didn't stop her from biting my hand—the first and only time she had ever done that. I have no explanation for her behavior. But it happened. For six years as a player and five as a coach, the Suns fed me well. Maybe Barkleigh's bite was a reminder that—despite my frustration and disappointment with Jerry and the Suns at that moment—don't bite the hand that feeds you?

Shortly after that, Cindy and I were invited to dinner at the home of our friends, Sharon and Dennis Dugan. Their good friend, actor Michael Keaton, was also there. He and his longtime girlfriend, Courteney Cox, had been all over the covers of the tabloids for several months, but he was there alone. This was no real surprise—because the breakup of America's couple-of-the-moment had just been announced.

Though the sting of my dismissal was not far from the surface, we were excited to meet Batman, and determined to be tactful about his pain. But … he spoke first!

"So how does it feel to be fired by the Suns?"

There was nothing wrong with his question or tone. He seemed like a really nice guy. But somehow this answer slipped out, "Probably about the same as being dumped by Courteney Cox."

It wasn't I who said it but Cindy.

There was a notable silence that followed until Sharon said, "Dinner is served." We took our places around the table as though nothing awkward had just happened. Leaving, buckling up in the car and pulling out of the Dugan driveway, Cindy looked at me, and asked, "Did I just think that, or did I say that out loud?"

Let's just say, we never saw Batman again.

When the Sacramento Kings fired me in 2011, I had almost given them no choice but to let me go. I suppose they could have decided to do the right thing, which would have been to support my efforts to discipline one of the most difficult and talented players I've ever been around, but the right thing is not always the best thing in the NBA.

DeMarcus Cousins had been doing things his way for his entire life. The party line of those who knew him was, "DeMarcus has a good heart. He just needs to mature."

I had said those exact words myself and tried my best to believe it too. But the "post-DeMarcus" analysis of those left in his wake was quite different. Without going into private detail, the self-described "misunderstood" large human being had a history of feeling unfairly treated and abused by referees, coaches, fans, media, police, teachers, bus drivers, teammates, strength coaches, and most importantly, I suspect, his father.

Anyone who tried to help him would be met with violent threats and wild mood swings. I was no different. When we drafted him, we all joked he was the kind of player who would either be a bust or an All-Star—for his third or fourth coach. As his first NBA coach, I would be a dead man walking, unless I could get him to change. Show confidence, patience, love, support, and truthfulness, mixed with clear lines of discipline and graduated consequences—that was the plan the organization agreed to follow.

Until they didn't.

The realities of professional basketball trumped our plan. When DeMarcus demanded a trade for the third time, only four games into the lockout-shortened 2011 season, I kept my word to both him and the Kings organization. I had promised Cousins and his agent that we could not keep his indiscretions behind closed doors. Fines and meetings had been tried, and public disclosure and suspensions would be part of future levels of consequences when he misbehaved.

After I explained the situation and received the proper organizational clearance (Kings President Geoff Petrie even suggested a word be changed, which I agreed made the statement read more clearly), I released a statement explaining DeMarcus' absence from the Arena for our game against the New Orleans Hornets. With Cousins not present, it was like oxygen had been pumped into our team's lungs! We enjoyed our most spirited and satisfying victory since the last time I had suspended him for a road game the previous season—when we upset the Steve Nash-led Phoenix Suns.

I'll never forget what Suns Coach Alvin Gentry whispered to me in the parking garage after that game. "I know I shouldn't say this, but I'm almost glad you beat us after suspending him. It's good for basketball when someone does the right thing."

Alvin had learned a lot from Larry Brown when he was Larry's assistant coach many years ago. I had witnessed Coach Brown argue with a referee for making a wrong call, even though the call benefited his team! You see, Larry cared more about the well-being and integrity of the sport than winning … which says a lot, because he cared very much about winning. Alvin Gentry, like Larry Brown, is a statesman in a world of politicians.

Kings' owner Gavin Maloof came into the coaches' office after we drilled New Orleans without our big center. "Congratulations, Coach!" he hollered. "I am so happy! Great win. Great win!"

"It couldn't have happened without you supporting the suspension," I responded. "Thanks for having my back!"

I had promised Kings' owners Joe and Gavin Maloof when I was being interviewed for the job that I would put the welfare of the organization ahead of my own—if we ever came to a crossroads where there might be a choice between doing what was best for the Kings or covering my butt, I'd choose the Kings. I felt like I had somehow done both that day.

I'm pretty sure that Cousins' agent made a late-night call to someone who could convince Gavin to see things differently. A meeting had been set for ten the next morning by Geoff Petrie that was to include me, Cousins, and his agent. The plan was DeMarcus would be given an opportunity to apologize to me, his teammates, the Kings organization, the fans, and all other offended parties for his unprofessional behavior. After that, we would forgive him and go to the airport to catch our chartered jet for a game in Denver.

I was in my office by 9:30.

When it got to be 10:15, I wandered down the hall to Geoff's office. The door was closed. Not unusual, especially if he was on the phone. "Let me know when DeMarcus and his agent get here, okay? I'll be in my office," I said to Petrie's assistant.

Of course, it burned me that Cousins would show up late, but it happens.

"They're in with Geoff now," I was told.

"Oh."

I knew that meant trouble. My fears were realized when Petrie appeared at my office door a few minutes later. By himself.

Geoff Petrie is as honest and honorable as anyone I have known in the NBA. He will tell the truth, even to his own detriment—or he will say nothing.

"I thought I was supposed to be in the meeting—" I began.

He shrugged and offered no explanation. He didn't have to. We both knew it hadn't been his decision. Someone from upstairs had changed the agenda.

"Geoff, how can he apologize if I'm not there?" I asked.

"He denies that he asked to be traded," Petrie responded. "He hated the press release. He says it's unfair to him. No apology, of course."

"I was hoping we could put this behind us and all get on the plane to Denver. Now what?"

"He's on the way to the airport. You should get going too," Petrie said.

"WHAT?"

"I know this is terrible, Paul, but we need to see what happens over these next two road games," Petrie said. "You don't have to start him, or even put him in the game."

"But I don't even want him around the team until he apologizes. He's calling me—his coach—a liar. He disrespected his teammates and the whole organization by demanding a trade, and now he gets to waltz back in with zero consequences? It sends the worst possible message!"

"I know. But he won't apologize. He says he didn't ask for a trade and that the whole thing is a big, unfair misunderstanding. How many times have we heard that one, huh?"

"Geoff, he and I were the only ones in my office when he said it, but Jim Eyen (my assistant coach) and several others heard him muttering about what he was about to say before we closed the door behind us. That he wanted to be traded. This is ridiculous. I am not making this up."

"I know, Paul. Nobody believes him. Everybody knows who's telling the truth. But he was told he can go on the trip. We'll see how things go and talk when you get back."

"Geoff, we both know I'm on the last year of my contract. I either need an extension or you should fire me right now. Any credibility I have in the locker room will be gone if you allow my authority to be undercut like this. How can the players respect me? Not to mention the damage it will do to DeMarcus if he's allowed to get away with this. You think he's a monster to deal with now? What do you think he'll be like if he can call his coach a liar and then go on to the next game?"

"We both know the Maloofs have a lot invested in him," Petrie said, "and currently his market value is zero. We can't trade him for anything we would want, and he won't back down. You know the owners are not about to spend any money now. They don't even know if they can remain as owners or keep the team in Sacramento. Nobody gets an extension now. Just try to talk to him on the plane and see how the trip goes."

"This is wrong."

"You better get going to the airport. Don't worry, he's not a good enough player to get someone fired."

My talk with Cousins on the plane was pathetic. I tried my best "let-us-reason-together" approach. He offered nothing as he slouched in his chair, avoided eye contact, and fiddled with his cell phone. I reminded him I was the one who pushed to draft him, and that I continued to believe in his talent and potential. I had promised him I would always deal with him truthfully, and that any discipline would be designed for his ultimate good. Shrugs and blank stares were about all he contributed to the conversation. When he did speak, it was so softly that his words were barely audible. When we got to Denver, the Nuggets beat us by about a million points. Then the Jazz duplicated the feat in Utah the next game. DeMarcus pouted the entire time, both on and off the court.

When we got back to Sacramento, I was called to Petrie's office. And not to sign an extension. I didn't think DeMarcus had improved over those last two games, but he must have, because he was now a good enough player to get his coach fired!

The day after I was relieved of my duties, I went to breakfast at my favorite little Sacramento breakfast dive. A nice young gal brought me coffee, blueberry pancakes, and a little perspective.

"Aren't you the coach of the Kings?" She beamed, eyes wide.

"I *was*. They fired me yesterday."

"Were you the coach when Omri Casspi was on the team?"

"Yes."

"He's cute!"

CHAPTER 3
NOBODY KNOWS ANYTHING

Looking back on the Sacramento years, I often wonder what I could have done differently, especially regarding the draft. But I believe there is an axiomatic truth that my years in coaching the Sacramento Kings underlined for me in red ink—"Nobody knows anything."

Sure, a person can be clever, well-informed, and experienced, but after events unfold and one looks in the rearview mirror, the uncertainty of the future humbles all honest analysts.

For example, Stephen Curry became the two-time MVP of the NBA. The Golden State Warriors' management had no idea that he could ever be that good. Nobody did. After the 2011–12 season the Warriors' brain trust decided that their two smallish guards, Curry and Monta Ellis, could not play together. So they made them available to be traded. Another team could pick either one. Ellis was a bit older and had proven to be a dynamic scorer, and Curry had shown flashes of charismatic brilliance tempered by balky ankles and a lack of physicality that made him a liability on defense. The Milwaukee Bucks chose Ellis and sent their talented but often-injured center, Andrew Bogut, West in exchange for the guard they preferred.

I believe Curry is probably the greatest shooter of all time—certainly the greatest when range and degree of difficulty are factored in. But when he was coming to the NBA out of Davidson College, one of the Kings' most experienced scouts, Scotty Sterling, questioned if Curry would ever be strong enough to shoot the longer NBA three-pointer consistently.

Nobody agreed with Scotty, but still.

There were a lot of great guard prospects in the 2009 NBA draft. Along with Curry, teams could choose between James Harden, Tyreke Evans, Ricky Rubio, Johnny Flynn, Ty Lawson, DeMar DeRozan, Darren Collison, Jrue Holiday, Jeff Teague, and Brandon Jennings. In hopes of sorting out who we would select with our fourth pick, we invited as many of them as would attend to work out together in Sacramento. James Harden was a cinch to be drafted prior to our pick, so he didn't come. Ricky

Rubio refused to compete against the others. To their credit, Curry, Flynn, Jennings, and Evans, plus a few more hopefuls we considered, showed up and went at each other. Tyreke Evans dominated the session like he was the varsity scrimmaging against the JV. The others couldn't get around him, and he went around (or through) anyone who tried to guard him. His shot was shaky, but shots improve with time. There was no question at all who the best player in the gym was when the workout ended.

With the fourth pick, we selected Tyreke Evans. Ricky Rubio and Johnny Flynn went to Minnesota at five and six, and then Steph Curry was taken by Golden State. We felt our pick was validated when Evans went on to be named Rookie of the Year. Curry finished the last couple of months strong, but the voting for the best rookie was never in doubt.

As their careers progressed, however, Curry kept improving while Evans was never able to match the success he enjoyed that first season. He had seemed almost indestructible with that six-foot-six, 230 pounds, not-an-ounce-of-fat prototypical NBA body of his. But he ended up being the more fragile player. How could anyone predict that? And his shooting didn't improve enough either. He worked on it. But it didn't happen. Meanwhile, Steph Curry's improvement is probably unmatched in the history of the League.

Nobody knows anything.

I have more proof.

The next season, we drafted DeMarcus Cousins with the fifth pick. Everyone knew he was the most talented player in the draft, but his ranking fell due to concerns about his attitude. Well-founded concerns. Even in selecting him, we weren't so naive as to believe I wouldn't be the first of many coaches he would get fired. But we were desperate for talent. With our second-round pick that season, I talked Mrs. Maloof, Joe and Gavin's mother and the real decision-maker when it came to money, into selecting another center, Hassan Whiteside.

She wanted to sell the pick, but I begged her to take Whiteside because of his great potential. Thankfully, she relented. He wasn't ready and wouldn't be for a few more years, but he turned into one of the most productive centers and highest-paid players in basketball. And then there was Isaiah Thomas, who we selected with the last pick of the second round the next year. He became an All-Star for the Boston Celtics. My point is that every team in the League passed on both of those guys.

Nobody knows anything.

Want more proof?

The same year we chose Isaiah Thomas, our first-round pick was Jimmer Fredette. Assistant Coach Keith Smart had been with Golden State for Steph Curry's early years. He told me Fredette would be a better pro than Curry. This wasn't as outlandish a statement as one might think. Fredette had credentials. He had been the leading scorer and NCAA Player of the Year at BYU. One memorable game versus San Diego State he was guarded by future all-pro Kawhi Leonard. Fredette dropped fifty in that game!

Needing a guard, we passed on Leonard, whose shot wasn't much better than Evans' had been at a similar stage, and selected Fredette. Looking back, that was an unthinkable choice—but he had dropped fifty on Leonard in a game that BYU won! Sure, there were concerns about his defense, as there are with many great scorers, but he was a high-character guy and a willing worker. And don't forget—he had dropped fifty on Kawhi Leonard!

So with almost identical credentials and scouting reports, and amazing charisma as well, Steph Curry went on to be a two-time MVP (and counting).

When the sportswriters and online blogging geniuses pass judgment on how the Kings' three drafts panned out during my time there, I wonder what they'll say. They might declare we drafted sensationally, claiming one Rookie of the Year and three future All-Stars. Or they could—and probably should—say that our performance was abysmal, having passed on Steph Curry, Klay Thompson, and Kawhi Leonard, ending up with only an underachieving small forward, a bust of a shooting guard, and a coach-killing center who gets stats, but never gets his teams to the playoffs. Hindsight pays well. But in real-time?

Nobody knows anything.

CHAPTER 4
CREDENTIALS FOR COACHING

I made my first basket the very day I was strong enough to heave the ball up and into the hoop my dad had mounted over the garage door for my brother, Bill, and me in our Redondo Beach, California, backyard. I had been trying every day for weeks, but from the time that first shot went in, I lived and breathed basketball. I got pretty good, too. Good enough to be one of a handful of guards in NBA history to shoot over fifty percent from the field for a career. Good enough to be a five-time All-Star, and four-time All-NBA. But the real way I've always felt certain I could play doesn't come from any of those kinds of honors. I knew I could play because Black players accepted me—as many players told me over the years—as a "bad White boy." Sorry P.C. crowd, but that's the truth.

I never expect to get recognized in public, but when you've been involved with the NBA as a player, coach, and broadcaster for nearly fifty years, it's not unusual to be recognized on the street. Still, I don't expect it. After all, not everybody loves basketball. But I don't believe I've ever *not* been recognized by a Black skycap at the airport. Often, they'll talk about how they, or their father, saw me play when I would go to Compton for pickup games while in high school. I might have been the only White guy on the floor, but my game was more "city" than "suburbs." They remember I took it hard to the hoop, often finishing with a dunk. If I'm proud of anything I've accomplished in basketball, I'm probably most proud of being able to compete with, and gain the respect of, Black athletes who have dominated basketball since the game was integrated.

I was incredibly moved to be inducted as a player into the Naismith Memorial Basketball Hall of Fame in 2019. Basketball holds no higher honor than that. The whole experience was amazing, not the least of it being inducted with Chuck Cooper (posthumously), Teresa Weatherspoon, and the iconic Tennessee State teams represented by Dr. Dick Barnett. As a historically Black school, racist policies prevented them from competing in the NCAA tournament. So the school known then as Tennessee A&I simply went out and won three NAIA national championships.

All of these inductees have a backstory of racial and gender obstacles that I never faced. Chuck Cooper, along with Nat "Sweetwater" Clifton and Earl Lloyd, combined to more or less simultaneously break the NBA color barrier. Teresa Weatherspoon had to fight her way through poverty, prejudice of many kinds, and people whose message was overwhelmingly negative and geared toward making her give up on her dreams. Dr. Barnett, a great player for both the Lakers and Knicks in the 1960s, spoke eloquently at the induction ceremony about the importance of education and the need for personal dedication to succeed.

In one of Dick's illustrations, he recalled spending his time alone in the gym working on his jump shot instead of attending his high school prom. I followed him to the podium and told everyone I could relate, because I had done the same thing! "But it wasn't because I was so dedicated," I said, "I just couldn't get a date." Though laughter followed my remarks, I found out after the speech that his point wasn't about dedication, so much as it was about the fact that as a Black man he wasn't allowed to attend the prom.

Easy for a White boy from Redondo Beach to assume, I suppose.

But I didn't miss the point on purpose. I held all of these inductees in high esteem, and I was thrilled they were finally being honored for their contributions to basketball and their impact on the very fabric of our nation. That's why I was quick to say "yes" when Chuck Cooper's son wanted to interview me for an upcoming documentary he was putting together about his father's life.

I was asked to contribute some comments regarding what I thought about breaking the color barrier. I answered that he and the other pioneers had helped turn the NBA into one of the best examples of a merit-based system that can be found in America. Because of Chuck Cooper and others, people from the inner-city, or a farm, someone from Redondo Beach, or even a player from some Communist Bloc country could come together and compete. And may the best man win! I went on to say that, in my view, in America, only Christianity had a bigger influence on fostering racial equality than basketball, and that everyone in our country should be very proud of his father and people like him.

In 2019, I also participated in another documentary, this one honoring the Compton High School teams of the late 1960s who won sixty-six consecutive games. Truly one of the greatest high school streaks ever—especially considering they didn't attract students from anywhere but the immediate neighborhood in those days. My Aviation High School team had been one of their victims, but I was remembered for scoring thirty-nine against them and our team almost upsetting them in the CIF (California Interscholastic Federation) playoffs.

I was blessed to be invited to a preliminary screening of the excellent film. Following the screening, a discussion took place. One of Compton's former players, Ron Richardson, stood and said, "I want to tell you a story. When Paul was in high school, he came over to Compton to play in some pickup games with us. One of our teammates said, 'I got the White guy.' Well, Paul scored eleven of his team's first thirteen baskets, and the guy who had asked to guard him said, 'Why don't you guys give me some help?' We answered, 'You said you wanted the White guy. Guard him yourself!'" Making the Hall of Fame didn't feel any better than hearing that story—more than fifty years after it happened.

When I was in my early fifties, my son, Michael, and I went out for some ice cream. His scoop slipped off the cone as he was walking to the table. So I sat to eat mine before it melted. He got back in line. While he waited, he overheard the man in front of him talking to his young son. "See that guy sitting over there by himself eating his cone? Believe it or not, he used to be a great basketball player." It was the "believe it or not" that killed me. Surely I wasn't *that* old. I didn't feel old. And I was pretty sure I could still dunk if you'd bet me enough.

I flashed back to the first time I met the greatest NBA coach of all time, Arnold "Red" Auerbach. The world was different then. These days, the top fifty or so prospective NBA draft choices are paraded around the country for various workouts, tryouts, and psychological evaluations for about a month and a half leading up to the draft. The top players are brought together in New York prior to draft day and fitted with $5,000 suits that would have cost them their college eligibility had a booster bought them a few months earlier. Then, after the NBA Commissioner calls their name, they come forward and put on the hat of the lucky team blessed enough to have selected their future star. ESPN runs a puff piece heralding the perfection of the fit for both player and team. And finally, the party starts.

When I was drafted 10th in the first round by the Boston Celtics in 1972, I thought I heard it mentioned on the radio, but I wasn't sure. So I went to bed. When morning came, I checked page five or seven of *The Los Angeles Times* sports section. I scanned the "Transactions" section, hoping to find the fine print listing of the previous day's NBA draft results. Sure enough, there it was! But what next? I didn't hear anything from either the League or the Celtics. You'd have thought someone would've called me or something.

True, I had suffered a career-threatening knee injury. I had been left on my own to rehab from Dr. Frank Jobe's surgery. I even fashioned a makeshift set of weights using my bride's makeup case, so I could strengthen my muscles while on our honeymoon in Hawaii. Still, the Celtics had decided to take a chance on me. But it was weird I hadn't heard from them.

Three days later, I received a telegram that had been forwarded to the USC basketball office. Even in 1972, telegrams shouldn't have taken four days. Red Auerbach's secretary, Mary Whalen, had sent it to Southern California College, not the University of Southern California. It congratulated me on being selected by the Boston Celtics and requested I call Mr. Auerbach—collect—to arrange a visit to Boston.

A few days later, I found myself being ushered on a tour of the Boston Garden by the cigar-chomping legend. It was June, but freezing cold, with dirty snow still visible on the streets. The trains made a squealing noise that sounded like a bag of fighting cats. Metal-on-metal, no grease. Eeeeeiiiiiieeeek! Red led me through the beat-up train station and up the stairs to the Celtics' run-down offices. His was home to his collection of letter openers from around the world. Hundreds of them. He showed me around the Garden, the greatest gym in history, where Russell and Cousy had played, where Havlicek and White and Cowens were about to lead the Green back to the top where they belonged. I could not have been more enthralled. It was like getting a private tour of the Vatican conducted by the Pope, only better. I'm not Catholic. But I was all about basketball, and this was basketball heaven. I remember telling myself to hang onto every word this man would say. After all, he was the architect of a championship dynasty that had won eleven of thirteen NBA World Championships. (This was the great Red Auerbach I was listening to, and no doubt, he would soon be gone. After all, the old man was over fifty. Just about my age when Michael dropped his ice cream.)

Red wasn't the coach of the Celtics during the three years I played in Boston. That was Tommy Heinsohn, a Hall-of-Famer. I also played for John MacLeod, who like fellow former Suns' coach and my revered mentor, Lowell "Cotton" Fitzsimmons, should be in the Hall of Fame, along with Lenny Wilkens, Red Holzman, and Hubie Brown. All Hall-of-Famers.

I played for a great coach every year of my career, but none surpassed Hubie Brown. One day he and I had a conversation I'll never forget. He was talking about all the "problem children" he'd coached.

"Hubie," I said, "I believe that I've coached more troubled individuals and/or substance-abusers than anyone in NBA history." Keep in mind that this was several years *before* I coached DeMarcus Cousins in Sacramento, so Hubie thought this might be a debatable statement.

"John Drew," said Hubie. Drew had arrived in the League directly from junior college, almost unheard of in those days, to star for Hubie's Atlanta Hawks. Later, he developed a drug problem that would derail his career. A heartbreaking tale, for sure.

"Richard Dumas," I replied without hesitation. As a rookie, Richard frequently had outplayed an in-his-prime Scottie Pippen in the 1993 NBA Finals. Substance abuse issues ruined his career soon after.

"Fast Eddie Johnson."

"Vin Baker," I shot back.

"Olden Polynice."

"Ha! I had OP too. Vernon Maxwell!"

"You must be forgetting that I had 'Mad Max' myself," Hubie stated.

"Ruben Patterson," I continued.

"Marvin 'Bad News' Barnes."

We went back and forth for several more turns until I brought out my heavy artillery. My trump card was a player who had been accused of having his pregnant girlfriend murdered because she wouldn't abort their child. He was never tried, but the person who was convicted of being the hired killer proclaimed his innocence by testifying the player had indeed contracted the killing—with someone else! And I had to keep the player on our team because he had a big contract that the team would be obligated to honor if we cut him before he was charged or convicted.

Hubie conceded the trophy to me.

The reason I mention this exchange is that during my seasons coaching the Seattle SuperSonics, I had six of the players I had used to defeat Hubie. Most NBA teams have at least one eccentric personality. One drama king can often be endured. Sometimes two, if coupled with a group of mature, strong-willed (and talented) veterans. But *six*? That's a ticket to unemployment for a coach. Still, while it lasts, a coach needs to be optimistic while trying to get through to his team. Great ones find a way—or at least go down swinging!

CHAPTER 5
GREAT MENTORS OBSERVED

Cindy thinks I swing for the fences too much. Ping-pong, golf, slow-pitch softball, tennis, whatever. What can I say? Like the famous 1999 Nike commercial said, "Chicks dig the long ball." So I take it as a compliment. If I played things safe, I never would have worked up the nerve to ask her to marry me.

So on a snowy night before a game in Denver, I decided to forgo our normal pre-game routine. Instead of a scouting video, chalk talk, and game-plan review, I decided to tell my Seattle SuperSonics team a story. I wanted to try to rekindle (or, in some cases, kindle) the love of what basketball ought to be to my troubled and cynical group. I gathered the team together and, for about half an hour, I told them the story of my first year of coaching—an improbable year that sounded like fiction. I'd tell them about a year I hoped would bring them to a place of humility and sacrifice, embracing a "team-first" attitude that can happen in basketball only a few times in a lifetime. But when it happens, it's sublime.

WILT VS. RUSSELL

Basketball is the ultimate "team" game. Contrast it to baseball. A great game, but baseball is a game for individuals who wear matching uniforms. Players take turns at bat. Everyone who is in the lineup figures to get their hacks three to five times per game. If they get a hit, no one says they are selfish. And someone who goes four-for-four often enough can be respected as a great player, no matter how bad his team might be.

But in basketball, every play contains decisions about whether to pass or shoot. A great player with selfish teammates will seldom find a good shot. Maybe he won't get the screens he should, or a pass might be delivered late. Star players on losing teams are often blamed, no matter what the stats say. Why? Because truly great players understand they are measured by how well they can make the team function.

That was one of the big differences between Wilt Chamberlain and Bill Russell. Wilt was the most dominant player ever. No one else was even close. He averaged over fifty points a game one season. Fifty! He also averaged more than forty-eight minutes one year, possibly the most untouchable record in basketball. After all, a game is only forty-eight minutes! And his team saved money by not needing a back-up center.

So why isn't Wilt acknowledged as the greatest of all time? Rings. Russell earned eleven, Wilt two. As a high-school kid, I once played in a pickup game with Wilt. I made a cut and he hit me with a pass for a wide-open 15-footer. A shot I could hit with my eyes closed, but I missed. It happens. Wilt stared at me with an expression of disgust. A few plays later, I found myself wide open in the same spot. He saw me, shook his head, and passed somewhere else. He made me feel like a chump. Russell was the opposite. He was encouraging and unselfish to his teammates. Because of that, they played with confidence, not to mention unselfishness. Teams follow the lead of the best players. Stats mattered little on Russell's teams, but they seemed to reign supreme on Wilt's. Russell wanted the wins, Wilt wanted the records. I'm not saying Wilt didn't want to win. But Russell was better because he knew how to win. Wilt should have played baseball. He would have been the greatest player ever!

Before I get to the story that I told my team in the Denver locker room, I need to provide some background. I had always figured I would be a basketball coach. Nearly all the coaches I'd been around had taught me things I felt a strong desire to pass along. X's and O's, of course. But more importantly, the love of playing the game the way it should be played.

COMITAS, HUGHES, AND BROWN

Nick Comitas was my first coach, at Lincoln Elementary School in Redondo Beach. He impressed my father, not only with his ethical priorities and love of kids, but that he was a detail-guy. He would check our fingernails before every game and clip them if they were too long. My dad loved the message of respect for opponents that this simple act of checking our nails sent. Coach Nick didn't just talk about caring, he thought of ways to show it. And my dad noticed.

Rex Hughes was another man whose influence on my life had a profound effect on my development. He later became a long-time college coach and NBA assistant coach and scout, even serving a hitch as interim head coach of the Sacramento Kings. But when I first encountered him, he was a recent college graduate who was refereeing elementary school games for the Redondo Beach Recreation Department. And I was a cocky, hot-tempered, sixth-grade scoring machine.

In our biggest game of the year, against the other undefeated team in the league, Beryl Street Elementary School, he was the official. Beryl's entire strategy was to rough me up. And they did a great job of it. They held me to a single basket, and Rex didn't send me to the line even once. Late in the game, I snapped. After an egregious, uncalled foul which resulted in a turnover, I chased the thief down from behind and kneed him in the butt.

Rex finally got a call right. He ejected me. But he didn't leave it at that. He sought me out after the game and told me that he also battled a temper, and that his inability to control it had hurt his playing career. "Unless you can learn to turn your temper into competitiveness, you will never reach your potential."

I took his advice to heart, much like tennis great Bjorn Borg took his mother's discipline seriously when she took his racquet away from him for six months when he burst into a tantrum over a bad call. Borg went on to become one of the most stoic, unflappable, yet focused competitors in the history of sports. Too bad DeMarcus Cousins never ran across either Rex Hughes or Mrs. Borg when he was twelve.

My high school coach, Ken Brown, was another man of character who set a wonderful example for his players. He was never blessed with tall teams. Never had anyone over 6'4", but they sure did scrap. Coach Brown worked us harder than we thought we could endure. But he treated everyone on the team with respect, and he encouraged us to never be afraid of making a mistake as long as we were being aggressive. He demonstrated to friend and foe alike how a true sportsman should compete.

During my senior year, I averaged 32.5 points per game, setting a California Interscholastic Federation record for points in a season. Coach Brown never let me run up my scoring totals though, sitting me out of at least fourteen entire quarters because we already had those games well in hand. I never regretted for one second him doing that. What good would a record be if the object of the game needed to be perverted to achieve it? Ken Brown had class.

STANICH

George Stanich is another coach who had a major influence on my life, even though I never played for his El Camino Junior College team. El Camino is located close to the 405 in Torrance. He made sure his gym was open and available, not just to his own players, but to anyone. He figured if he could make his gym the place great players competed, his team could only benefit from the exposure to a higher level. Since El Camino was easily accessible to people from the basically White South Bay, as well as to those who lived in the predominantly Black Compton area, it was a perfect place for all who loved basketball to interact.

George was John Wooden's first player to be named All-American at UCLA, as a defensive specialist, no less. There is an oft-repeated story regarding a game UCLA played against USC in 1950. I've heard an account of the game personally from John Wooden, Bill Sharman, George Yardley's son, Rob, and George Stanich himself—and they all agree.

The great Hank Luisetti's conference scoring record was threatened by both George Yardley and Bill Sharman on the last day of Pacific Coast Conference play. Yardley and his Stanford team played an early game, and he did score enough to set a record. Sharman went into the game against the Bruins knowing how many points he needed to make Yardley's record last but a few hours, and he intended to do so. George Stanich, assigned to check the future Hall-of-Famer, had different ideas. The very first time a USC player set a screen to try and free Sharman for a shot, Stanich lowered his shoulder and ran right through the screen. Before the obliterated Trojan hit the floor, Stanich raised his hand in agreement with the official who was calling the foul on him, as if to say, "I did it, sir. I bet that hurt. I've got four more fouls just like that for anyone who gets in my way."

At a reunion of the old El Camino crowd I attended in 2016, the eighty-seven-year-old coach fondly recalled the moment. "That first guy who set the screen, I knocked him on his A-double-S real good. After that, it just seemed like their players were leaving me enough room to get through those screens."

Indeed. He held Sharman without a field goal for the entire first half. But when UCLA opened a sizable lead early in the second half, Coach Wooden removed his defensive star for the remainder of the game. Basketball is not an individual game, after all, and Wooden couldn't care less if Sharman got the record. As Stanich sat steaming on the bench, Sharman went on to set the new conference scoring record. Believe me when I tell you, Stanich never did forgive John Wooden for removing him. And neither did George Yardley's mother. Every time she was in the presence of Coach Wooden for the rest of her life, she made it a point to go up to him and chastise him for removing Stanich from the game, depriving her son of the PCC scoring record.

Coach Stanich also won an Olympic bronze medal in the 1948 games for the high jump, as well as enjoying a brief professional baseball career as a pitcher. I didn't know about any of that then. All I knew—from the time I was a skinny little sophomore at Aviation High until I stopped spending summers in Los Angeles after I'd been in the NBA for a few years—was that his gym would be open at 6:30 on Tuesday and Thursday evenings and every Saturday morning at 9:00 sharp. The best players from the area would be there, and anyone could sign up for a game. Even fifteen-year-old me.

The way it worked was to get there early. Not on time—early. Get your name on that list. Second, if possible, bring ringers. That's because losing was not an option. There were four baskets designated by Coach Stanich and his assistant, Kelly Kappen. When your group's turn came, your team would face off on the side court for a game of three-on-three. The first team to 11 (by ones) wins. Shirts vs. skins. Not the way it is today, when nobody wants to take their shirt off, so you can't tell one team from another. Shirts against skins! If you lost on Court #4, you might as well head home. Sometimes the good players might get picked up. But skinny sophomores from Aviation didn't get chosen after their name got scratched off the list.

If you got a win on Court #4, you still weren't done yet. As the losers slinked off, the winners would move up to Court #3 for a game against the loser on Court #2. If you happened to lose a Court #3 game, just like a Court #4 game, you'd be done. Winners moved up, losers were out! It's called competition.

Once a team arrived on the main Courts, #1 and #2, there was a little more wiggle room. If a team lost there, they'd slide down. Wins on Court #1 made you feel like Heavyweight Champ Joe Louis felt with his "Bum of the Month" club. He was the champ, and after he dispatched a challenger, he would assume the boxing equivalent of El Camino's Court #1 and get ready for the next bum. As I grew and got better—and played with a higher class of ringers—I would sometimes be able to hold Court #1 from 6:30 until closing. But rarely.

I never missed open gym at El Camino. Even during the basketball season, I'd go home for dinner after practice and show up at El Camino before 6:30. When I needed to take Driver's Education, much to my chagrin, I found it was only offered on Saturday mornings. I was afraid I'd have to skip playing if I wanted to get my license. But a beautiful thing happened. My Driver's Ed teacher was Ken Brown, my high school coach! We'd meet at Aviation at 8:30, drive the fifteen minutes it took to get to El Camino, and practice parallel parking until the gym opened. Then we'd drive back at 1 o'clock. I got an "A" too!

Going undefeated on Saturday was a feat for the ages. Three-on-three happened from 9 until 11 a.m. Then the two three-man teams from Court #1 would each add a couple of guys to their squad for full court games. Winners stay, losers out! This would go until one in the afternoon, so to go undefeated on Saturday, we had to go for four hours against the best players Los Angeles had to offer. Even when I was a pro and able to stack my team with guys like ten-year NBA pro John Block and my old high school teammate Garrick Barr (the best screen-and-roll player I ever knew), sweeping a Saturday was almost impossible.

Pickup basketball can get messy. Anyone who's ever played knows how "call your own fouls" can dissolve a friendly game and turn it into a war. Or even worse, no more game. Tempers, integrity, and "losers-go-home" is a volatile mix. That's where George Stanich came in. No profanity or arguing was allowed in his gym. He didn't referee the half-court games (those were on the honor system, and players who couldn't abide by that would be banished), but he did preside over the five-on-five full court contests. If a player complained, he soon learned that the next few calls would go against him. If things started to *really* get out of hand, George would blow the whistle to gather everyone at half court. "You know, I gave up my whole morning for you. I could be home loving my darling wife, but I'm here instead. And I'll be darned if I will keep opening this gym if you won't respect this game and your opponents. Are we clear?"

After all these years I can't remember his exact words, but those are pretty darn close. That's how he talked. It didn't hurt that behind his soft, non-cussing voice was a chiseled specimen that every person in the gym knew would be the last man standing if things ever got physical. He didn't have to say it. But the players all knew. Law and order reigned at El Camino.

Things are different for young players today. We learned to play by competing every chance we got. If the gym was closed, I'd play outside at the park or my backyard. If I was the only one there, I could practice shooting and ball-handling. If another arrived, we'd play one-on-one. Three people meant a game of two-on-one, with two players guarding whoever had the ball. Four players meant a two-on-two game, and so on.

Youngsters had to learn how to fit in with the older kids and developed into more well-rounded and less specialized players. Generally, today's kids play by appointment only, almost exclusively with their own age group. A power forward on the seventh-grade team is likely to remain a power forward all the way through high school, because he is destined to compete against the same people year after year. If there isn't an organized practice or game, most won't play. Oh, they might lift weights or work with a personal trainer or a shooting coach. But compete? When I was an assistant coach to Lionel Hollins with the Brooklyn Nets in 2015, we tried to encourage one of our rookies to play more one-on-one. He told us what we'd already observed: "Nobody plays one-on-one anymore."

Well, they ought to!

WOODEN, AUERBACH, AND CARRIL

While at Aviation High, I received recruiting feelers from virtually every school in America. I never considered leaving Los Angeles, so I narrowed my choice to either John Wooden's UCLA or Bob Boyd's USC. I set out to learn everything I could about each. Let's face it—pretty much everyone reveres Coach John Wooden. He remains a *bona fide* American icon. It is one of the greatest blessings of my life to have known him. The reality of who he was as a man dwarfs his stellar reputation. Who else can have *that* said about them? Evangelist Billy Graham? Sure. Who else?

I had my first contact with him when I attended the John Wooden Basketball School ("school" not "camp"!) in 1964, prior to my freshman year of high school. At one point, he pulled me aside and asked if I would mind listening to a suggestion he had. "Would I mind?"

Of course, I wanted to know what he had to say. And I've never forgotten.

"Paul, I know people often talk about gaining an advantage by taking a long first step. It appears that you have fallen into the trap of believing that a long first step is desirable. But consider this: when a sprinter comes out of the starting blocks, does he take long strides or short, choppy steps? They are short and choppy because it's a quicker way to get started, and quickness is the most important attribute a basketball player can possess. At some point, the stride should lengthen to reach maximum speed, but speed and quickness are not the same thing. There is a place for both, but quickness comes first."

That kind of insight poured from Coach Wooden. And as insightful as he was about basketball, he was many times more insightful about life. More John Wooden stories will come later, but let's first deal with the question I am always asked when people find out I chose to attend another university instead of Wooden's UCLA. There are many facets to that answer, not the least of which was that Coach Wooden had already hit fifty! Like Red Auerbach, he only had about forty or fifty good years of life ahead of him, but from my teenage perspective, he was ancient. Later in life, like Mark Cuban, I predicted that Steve Nash, at age thirty-two, couldn't have much great basketball left in him. And unless you count a couple of MVP awards, Mark and I were right. I don't have any other biases that I'm aware of, but I'm pretty sure I haven't always been on the correct side of the age-discrimination issue.

Years later, while serving the Sacramento Kings as my mentor and assistant coach, the great Pete Carril (eighty at the time—you see, I did eventually learn the value of experience!) shared an insight concerning the virtues of speed. It went hand-in-hand with what I had picked up from Coach Wooden, who had coined the phrase, "Be quick, but don't hurry." Only Pete liked to be a bit more colorful in his teaching:

"Three guys were sitting on a bench. A regular guy was sitting between the strongest man in the world and the fastest man in the world. The fastest guy reached around and snatched the hat right off the head of the strongest as he was napping. The middle guy gasped and said, 'Hey, buddy, don't you know that guy can crush you? He's the strongest man in the world. You must be nuts to grab his hat like that.' To which the man, who now had a new hat, said, 'Tell him the fastest guy in the world has his hat.'"

Legendary coaches John Wooden, Red Auerbach, and Pete Carril share many common traits. Unselfish basketball was the only basketball they could stomach. They all valued quickness over size. They were principled, but pragmatic. They possessed both great humor and great intensity. They liked and respected their players, but understood there had to be a line drawn between them. Like Yankee immortal Casey Stengel, they realized they "couldn'ta done it without the players." I was blessed to be able to spend priceless, meaningful time with every coach.

I was with the Celtics for three years, which means I heard every one of Red's stories three times. One of his favorites was about how he treated Bill Russell. He knew Bill hated practice, and unlike his teammates, didn't need much of it. Often the great center would sit with his legs crossed, reading the paper while the others scrimmaged. One day Sam Jones had enough, so he stormed off the court and took a seat next to Russell. He was challenging Red, and that could not stand.

Auerbach blew his whistle and the team, minus Russell, gathered around. "You guys know why we have all those banners? Because of that guy!" He nodded in the direction of his studious center. "I'm not saying that you guys are horse-(bleep), but you don't win without him, and you know it. I say he needs to rest, and I say you need to scrimmage. If you don't like it, too bad. It's not my job to keep you happy. It's your job to make me happy, so shut up and get back to work."

After they had gone up and down the floor a few times, Russell looked up from his reading. "Way to hustle, Sam," he said, and then returned to his paper.

Red hadn't given Russell a free ride, though. He knew when to call in a debt. One night the management of the St. Louis Hawks ran a promotion where they passed out cigars to all the men in the crowd. Red was famous for lighting up a victory cigar on the bench after the Celtics had put away a game. The plan was for the St. Louis fans to mock Auerbach by lighting up when the Hawks prevailed.

"Russell," he said, "if you let them light those cigars, you're never missing another practice." It was his entire pre-game talk. There were several thousand unlit cigars in St. Louis that night.

The Celtics locker room at the Boston Garden was pathetic. For the time I was there, no more than two of the six shower heads ever worked on the same day. Russell's grandfather, not far removed from a personal memory of how slavery had touched his world, traveled north to Boston to see his grandson play during his rookie year. After they won, he was invited into a clubhouse filled with celebrating Celtics. The usual post-win hijinks were on display with the joyful victors, as some showered and others dressed while basking in the satisfaction of another victory. Russell was surprised to see tears streaming down the face of his honored guest as he sat taking it all in.

"Is everything okay?"

"I'm fine. I could never imagine I would live to see the same water running off the backs of both races in this country. Yes, Bill, I'm very fine."

So when players used to complain about the terrible facilities at the Garden—and it truly was a dump—Red would always answer, "It was good enough for Russell. It's good enough for you, too."

I didn't play much, especially my rookie year. Since rookies weren't allowed to shower before the vets, I always had some time to kill before my cold shower. Before entering, I would stop off at the urinal. Red would come stand next to me and take care of his business at the same time. Cigar in his mouth for safety as he relieved himself, he would take the time to share some of his wisdom with me. It would be something simple like, "Keep your head up, kid. We don't play rooks here, but your time will come. Did you see how Havlicek took his time once he got DeBusschere on his back? Sometimes you hurry too much. Slow down and take advantage of your position when you get it." His comments were encouraging, simple, and useful. A little at a time.

Truth be told, despite their twenty-plus years' age difference, Cindy would have dumped me flat for Pete Carril if he had asked her to. She and about a million other girls. He and Cindy shared a love for Broadway. All she had to do was ask, and he would break into song for her. Thankfully, he allowed me to keep my happy home. He and I would have lunch together before every Kings road game. We'd talk about everything, sometimes even basketball. Like Red, he loved his cigars. When Pete was a young coach, he used to work Red's camp. Auerbach could be gruff and intimidating, but Pete wanted to find a way to ingratiate himself with Red so he could get close enough to learn from the master.

"Hi, Mr. Auerbach, would you like a cigar?"

Red looked disdainfully at the inexpensive stogie. "I don't smoke that sh—. Here, have one of mine."

Years later, Pete was head coach at Princeton, but still wasn't quite sure Red knew who he was. They were at Madison Square Garden for a college doubleheader when Pete realized he had run out of cigars. And it was time for a smoke. He'd never asked Auerbach for anything, but he wanted one of Red's fine cigars. So he walked up to him, cigar-less, and asked, "Hi, Red. Would you like a cigar?" as he pretended to reach into his inside pocket for a smoke.

"Naw. I don't smoke that sh—. Here, have one of mine."

John Wooden didn't smoke cigars, but he did eat. When UCLA recruited me in 1967, we went to dinner at the Velvet Turtle in Redondo Beach. Even though I chose USC, we stayed in touch. He always honored me by saying I was "the one who got away" that he regrets the most. He even got me out of jury duty once, not that he meant to.

While I was coaching at Pepperdine, I was summoned downtown to be in the jury pool for a murder trial. We were instructed that no one should expect to be excused, but I, like at least half of the 200-plus people in the pool, asked out anyway. Only two were granted their wish before Juror No. 237 (that was me) was called forward for a sidebar with the judge and the attorneys for both sides.

I arrived at his perch and nervously leaned in, so I could hear the judge's lowered voice. "About thirty years ago, I had a job in Parking Services at UCLA to help earn tuition money. Coach Wooden came to my window one day to renew his parking pass. I asked him how he thought we'd do against SC that night. He said, 'They have a kid named Westphal who is pretty good at moving without the ball. If we do a good job on him, I think we'll do fine.' I just wanted to tell you that. You're dismissed."

Not only did my connection with Coach Wooden get me out of jury duty, I can always say that—like Johnny Cochran—I participated in a sidebar with Judge Lance Ito, O.J. Simpson's judge.

Over the years, Keith Erickson, defensive anchor of UCLA's first two NCAA championship teams, would occasionally take me with him for visits to Wooden's home. Once we had a room full of very wise men figuratively sitting at the great man's feet. Pastor Ken "Hutch" Hutcherson was there, along with Pastor John Werhas (former Dodger and USC basketball player) and "The Sage of South Central" Larry Elder. Larry is a radio host and author, the kind of wise man whose respected advice is sought on all manner of topics. The pastors are both people whose wisdom is well-renowned. And Hutch (a former NFL linebacker) was one who was often called upon by Rush Limbaugh for advice on his radio program. And not just about football, either.

"I have a problem. I'd like to pick your brains," I said. "I have a player who collapsed at practice one day. We thought it was something simple, maybe he was dehydrated or had skipped a couple of meals. But it turned out to be a heart problem. Some doctors say he should never play again. Some say that after the procedure he had he should be fine. His mother is a doctor, and she is okay with him playing since he is committed to returning. They understand the risk, but I'm not sure if I should be onboard for this. Other schools will take him, but he could die if it happens again. What should I do?"

Silence.

I continued, "Keith, what do you think?"

"Hmm."

"John?"

Silence.

"Hutch? Larry?"

Then we all looked at Coach Wooden. We knew his would be the wisest response. We weren't disappointed.

"Is he a good player, Paul?"

"Yes, Coach."

After a pause, the great man continued, "Then, I'm glad it's your problem and not mine."

When it was time to go, he asked all of his guests to take a case of bottled water with them. He had stacks of it near his front door.

"No, Coach, we don't want to take your water, but thanks."

"You don't understand. Please take some. Ron Von Hagen, one of my former students"—two-man beach volleyball legend, one half of the Von Hagen-Ron Lang team—"distributes this and sends me a case every month. I've been drinking out of the tap for ninety-five years. I'm not going to change now."

Another time, I happened to stop in at Knott's Berry Farm to enjoy some of Mrs. Knott's famous fried chicken. As I was about to leave, I saw Coach Wooden and three companions being escorted to a table across the room. I didn't want to interrupt them, but I called their waitress over, paid their check, and left a note before I slipped out. The note said, "Thirty-five years ago, you bought me dinner at the Velvet Turtle. Now we're even."

The next day, I had a voicemail waiting for me at my office. In his best attempt at a disguised voice, he said, "I was at Knott's Berry Farm yesterday and saw someone who looks like you skip out on the check. Unless you pay today, the authorities will be at your door tomorrow." Then he hung up. When I stop and take stock of thrills in my life, receiving a crank call from the great man as he closed in on the century mark ranks right near the top of the list.

When Coach Wooden was in his early nineties, he graciously accepted my invitation to come out to Pepperdine University so he could watch practice and speak to our team. That was the plan, but mostly, he signed his books and posed for pictures. He did get a break from signing when he addressed our team, along with several dozen other athletes who heard he was there and didn't want to miss what he would have to say. For more than an hour, he held everyone's attention. His recall was amazing. He remembered details of games that took place more than sixty years earlier, sharing his timeless principles and wisdom. Then he took questions. There have been many books written by and about him. Any of them could give one a feel for what he was all about, but seeing and hearing him in person was one of those rare experiences in life that everyone who was there will cherish as long as they live.

As I was driving him back to his modest condo in Encino, he asked me, "Paul, I've always wondered what the real reason is that you chose to attend USC over UCLA in 1968?"

"Coach, I've been answering that question for almost forty years now. Sometimes I make a joke and say it would have taken me five years to graduate from UCLA—four years of schooling and a year trying to find a place to park."

"Yes. I know. I chuckled at that line when I first heard John Stewart of the Kingston Trio say it on their 'College Concert' album. I think that was 1961 or '62." Well, maybe he didn't say that, but he had heard me use the crack that I had lifted from the record many times. He wanted more—and deserved more. After all, he had offered me a chance to play in my hometown for the greatest coach and college dynasty in history, and I had chosen to matriculate across town instead. Not only that, when his great assistant coach, Jerry Norman, had come to my house to take me to dinner the night before the letter of intent signing day, I informed him I wouldn't be going to dinner because I had made up my mind to attend USC. When pressed to reconsider, I quoted Coach Wooden. "Coach advised me that once a person makes a decision, he should stick to it and make it work. If one is constantly thinking his decision was wrong, he won't learn to work his way out of tough situations. Quitting allows a person to become an excuse-maker."

Once I told Coach Norman that, there wasn't much else he could say. But now the old legend, who had always graciously acknowledged me as the "one who got away," wanted the real story. How could I refuse?

"I've explained many times that I believed it would be a greater accomplishment if we could beat UCLA, interrupting your dynasty and helping to start a new one across town at USC. I'd always admired John McKay's SC football program and dreamt of helping Trojan basketball reach similar heights."

"I accept that, but I still think there's more," the wise man answered. I might as well have tried to hold something back from Rex Stout's famed 1934 detective, Nero Wolfe. Or perhaps even Sherlock Holmes.

"Coach, I have never articulated this publicly, but there is more. Wicks and Rowe. I couldn't imagine myself as their teammate."

Sidney Wicks and Curtis Rowe were two of the greatest players in the country, but they also had some issues that, in my opinion, would keep them from ever accepting me onto "their" team. The truth is, I saw the game differently—both on and off the court. I'd also learned in my experience as a kid playing pickup ball with Wilt Chamberlain—being passed over because I'd missed a shot—respect among teammates was important to me.

A big part of John Wooden's genius was that he could maintain his integrity while still getting the most out of difficult players. His players respected the fact that he had "The Hammer," and wasn't afraid to use it. Legendary Marquette coach Al McGuire was once asked what he would do if he saw his star player walking down the street with a six-pack of beer the night before a game. "I'd duck into a doorway and hope he didn't catch me seeing him," was Al's pragmatic answer. If John Wooden would have handled similar situations the same way, he never tipped his hand.

One year, the best player in the NCAA—maybe of all time—was Bill Walton. As the oft-told story goes, Bill decided he wanted to wear his hair at a length he knew was unacceptable to Coach Wooden. After all, he was a man—The Man. So why shouldn't he assert his dominance?

"Bill, our first practice is about to begin, and your hair is too long to fit in with the standards I have established for our team. I know you are a man of principle, and I respect that. But so am I, so I'm sure that you will respect that my principles won't allow you to play on our team unless you get a haircut. We will miss you, Bill."

As Walton bolted to the training room for scissors, Bruin Athletic Director J.D. Morgan was aghast. He took issue with his employee, saying, "Coach. We *need* Walton!"

"Then let's hope he cuts his hair," Coach said.

Years later, Walton asked Coach Wooden if he would have banished him for refusing to cut his locks. "The important thing, Bill, is that you believed I would." That is what "The Hammer" is—the ability of a coach to enforce discipline and not get fired. He won two NCAA championships with Wicks and Rowe as his stars, never ceasing in his quest to teach all his players everything he could about life and basketball. His Christian faith and ideals ruled every part of his life. Coach Wooden was an insightful, idealistic pragmatist who also displayed sly humor as he taught.

After pausing a beat to absorb what I admitted to him about my decision, he smiled as he said, "Paul, I can understand that."

BOYD

Despite the obvious iconic coaching greatness I passed up by turning down Coach Wooden, I never regretted attending USC and playing for Bob Boyd. A person must make choices in life, and sometimes there are no wrong answers. Just different roads. Coach Boyd built a program that had us ranked No. 1 in the nation midway through my junior year. We finished 24–2, No. 2 in both the nation and Los Angeles! We started the next season at the top of the polls, but lost four of our top seven players (including me, torn cartilage and ligaments in my left knee) to various surgeries, so no one will ever know how different SC basketball history would have been if we had stayed out of the hospital, and Coach Boyd had been able to play out the hand he'd worked so hard to put together.

Bob Boyd taught me some very important lessons, too—some about basketball, but mostly about life. He focused his teaching on improving my defense, with what many would call mixed results. His practices were the most difficult I've ever experienced, and his defensive demands were relentless. His approach was what I needed, both on and off the court.

PAPPY

Nick Comitas, Ken Brown, John Wooden, Bob Boyd—all lived and coached in such a way that made me think that becoming a basketball coach would be the ideal way to make a positive difference and a living at the same time. But my biggest earthly influence toward becoming a coach, by far, was a man who never coached a game in his life. Meet my dad, Armin "Pappy" Westphal.

We called him "Pappy" after Pappy Yokum, Li'l Abner's father. Not because of any resemblance, but because he used to sit me on his lap every Sunday and read me the funny papers. Al Capp's Li'l Abner was our favorite, and somehow, we started calling him "Pappy." Our mother, Ruth, "nacherly" got stuck being called "Mammy."

If you asked for something, his first answer was always "no." But he probably meant "yes."

He always wore a white collared shirt with the sleeves rolled up. I think he had about five of them. After he retired, he mixed in some plaids.

He showed me the right way to play various games, but he never corrected me beyond my present ability to learn. I never knew it, and he *never* did admit it, but he always let me win. Until I grew taller than he was, and he could no longer beat me. But then it was too late. I think!

He paid me $5 to memorize Rudyard Kipling's "If."

He paid me a dollar for home runs and a quarter per base for hits in Little League. He should have taken a quarter back every time I walked a batter. He could have retired earlier if he had.

We never missed Sunday School.

It wasn't okay to place anything on top of his (or any) Bible.

He hated to have authority over others, but he accepted when asked to be both Sunday School Superintendent and President of North Redondo Little League. He organized each impeccably, doing all the work himself unless someone volunteered to help.

As an aeronautical engineer, he turned down any promotion that would require him to hire or fire people.

He never missed work. He got home at 5:20 every day.

He spanked me when I needed a spanking, but never in anger. If Mammy thought I needed to be spanked, but he saw a way to teach me without the swat, he would take me into another room, hit the bed, and tell me to holler. Then I'd return, rubbing my eyes, and give her a hug. She was probably in on it, too, now that I think about it.

People who didn't know him were often intimidated by his demeanor. No one who got to know him ever had anything but respect for him. He could be viewed as stern. But in truth, he was shy.

I can't remember him buying anything for himself.

He loved Cindy because he saw love toward me in her eyes. That sealed their bond ... period.

He couldn't resist a dog. He would share half of his steak with our dog, slyly slipping her bites under the table throughout the meal. You couldn't get him to admit it, though.

He never forced me to play or practice any sport, and he never refused when I would ask him to play or practice with me.

He didn't own a pair of shorts or sandals. No sunglasses either.

He would keep a scorebook for all the games my brother and I played. That way, he couldn't afford to put it down and go straighten out the refs.

I never heard him swear. "You no-good so-and-so," muttered under his breath if some driver committed a traffic offense, was about as bad as his language got.

He loved Suns' trainer Joe Proski. The Prosk had a mouth on him, but he was a hard worker and he liked me. Joe liked Pappy a lot, too, and watched his language as best he could out of respect.

He was saved at Harry Hank's Bible class, studying the book of Revelation.

If he ever complained, I never heard him.

He would always know if I could use a twenty and would find a way to slip one my way.

He would rather die than be a burden to someone. Probably did, too.

For safety, he would have me ride in the back seat. Unless I sat on his lap and steered.

The hoop and backboard he built over our garage was the best homemade setup I have ever seen.

He gave up wine, flying, motorcycles, softball, and golf for his family. Probably cigars, too. He never expressed regret about any of them. But I suspect his incurable hook made it easier to quit golf.

Don't even start to imagine that he ever turned down a piece of See's Candies.

If someone in his family started to get the sniffles, he'd slice up an orange, top it with powdered sugar, and make sure it was eaten. No negotiations.

If he thought another family member wanted a certain food item, he'd starve before grabbing it for himself.

He wore a watch and his wedding ring. No jewelry. When he went bald, he took it like a man.

He wouldn't steal so much as a pencil from work if it didn't belong to him.

He never told someone who he was. He showed them. And he always delivered more than he promised.

That was my dad. My greatest example and mentor.

CHAPTER 6
ROUGH START IN SEATTLE

I always tried to honor those who instilled in me a love of competition in general, and basketball in particular. By sharing the story of my first coaching position, I hoped this cynical SuperSonics team might find a reason to appreciate the concept of unselfishness and competing for reasons greater than individual compensation or renown. They needed this lesson more than any group I had ever been around. And they had no idea I was about to ask them to emulate the least physically gifted basketball team I had ever experienced.

I should have figured there was trouble ahead when I was hired as the SuperSonics' coach in 1998. After Charles Barkley had helped me achieve what was nearly the highest winning percentage in NBA history over my three-plus seasons as Suns' coach, I never doubted I would get another crack at coaching in the League. There just hadn't been a good fit for me for two full years after being fired in Phoenix, but I counted that time as a blessing. After all, I was still getting paid by the Suns, and I got to use the time to spend with my family and work as a volunteer assistant coach to Terry Kearney at Chaparral High School in Scottsdale. That's where our son, Michael, was about to play his junior and senior years. It would be irreplaceable time spent with my son, a great coach, and a great team. I got to attend every practice and game for two seasons. And as Terry's assistant, passing out playing time wouldn't be my job, so "favoritism" toward Michael, either real or perceived, wouldn't be a concern.

Not too long after Michael's senior season ended, two opportunities emerged to return to the bench in the NBA. One was with the Clippers, the other with Seattle. Since the SuperSonics were coming off a 61-win season, and the Clippers were mired in their usual "Clipper-ness," I was excited to head north to Seattle. After all, even though Shaq's Lakers had eliminated them 4–1 in the Western Conference semifinals, they seemed to have a great future. Coach George Karl had presided over a successful and exciting era in Seattle. But his contract had not been renewed, and it looked like a dream situation awaited me. Usually, NBA coaching jobs only open because the team has done poorly and somebody, especially the coach, must go. Whether it's the coach's fault or not, that's the way it goes. But this job seemed like a "ready-to-win" situation with youngish, in their prime All-Stars Gary Payton and Vin Baker shaping up as the next coming of John Stockton and Karl Malone. Talk about looks being deceiving!

I soon found out that George Karl had left town just in the nick of time.

The 1998–99 season got a very late start due to the owners locking the players out until January 1999. That meant there could be no contact between the new SuperSonics' coach—me—and the players. It was several months between the time I was hired and the lockout being lifted. I had been hired a mere day or two before the moratorium on communication between management and players was implemented, but I arranged to meet with Payton and his agent, Aaron Goodwin, during the brief interim. That one meeting served as a preview of the rocky road ahead. It was set for a restaurant in Oakland's Jack London Square. Gary arrived almost two hours late, without either a call or an apology. If I had it to do over again, I would have left after a half hour had passed, but this would be our only chance to meet for months, so I waited. I looked forward to talking basketball and getting to know my star player, but Gary didn't seem very interested in my agenda. I'm still not sure why he even showed up. He remained aloof while his agent did most of the talking and the subject he picked was—Rush Limbaugh.

I have never been one to let politics infringe on friendship. Like an overwhelming number of children of the 1960s, I had tended to lean a bit left in my late teens and early twenties. Until I realized that even though liberal policies sounded nice, they just made things worse for everyone. Liberalism didn't work, even for those it claimed to be trying to help. I understood those Founding Fathers were awfully wise. I came to agree with Mark Twain's comment, "There is no distinctly American criminal class—except Congress."[2] Since I don't trust people who got to where they are in life by promising more than they can deliver, or even by lying, I prefer smaller government and a strong national defense. Like our Founders. And Rush. I acknowledge there are many well-meaning people spread across

---

2 "Just a Moment …" Inspirational Quotes at BrainyQuote. Accessed June 18, 2024. https://www.brainyquote.com/quotes/mark_twain_137913.

the political spectrum, but I still agree with P.J. O'Rourke when he pointed out that giving money to politicians is like giving whiskey and car keys to teenage boys. Ultimately, politics fade in importance as we pass through this life. It's what is in our hearts that we all must deal with before we head into eternity.

One can detect duplicity in people on either side of the political fence, but I have often noticed that the "tolerant" left tends to be most intolerant when it comes to evaluating Rush. Personal attacks from people who don't listen to what he said are aimed at him daily. Rush was a big boy who could hold his own in an exchange of ideas, but no one could be untainted by mischaracterizations and name-calling. Aaron was predisposed to misjudge Rush as some kind of bigot, and I did my best to explain that if I believed that to be the case, I would have nothing to do with him. But I knew Rush to be the exact opposite of a bigot. Instead, I knew him to be a person who embraced Dr. Martin Luther King Jr.'s vision of a world where people are evaluated not by the color of their skin, but by the content of their character. So I spent some time explaining my relationship with Rush, instead of talking basketball.

One of my closest and most trusted friends is Mike Lupica, the outstanding best-selling author, radio and television personality, and *New York Daily News* columnist. Incidentally, Mike's politics are far to the left of mine, but he is the one who introduced me to Rush. He knew I admired the pro-life stance that Rush articulated and how he mixed a great sense of satire and humor into his political discourse. So when Limbaugh and Lupica met in the press box at a New York Giants football game, Mike dialed my number and handed the phone to the self-proclaimed "most dangerous man in America."

As we talked, we realized that we shared some mutual acquaintances. One of his good friends was baseball great George Brett. I had competed against both of his brothers, Bobby and Ken. Growing up, Ken was known as "Kemer." They were raised in El Segundo, the next town over from my home. Kemer had played a large role in helping me decide to pursue basketball instead of baseball. Until I hit the ninth grade, I wasn't too sure what my best sport was. But Bart Johnson, Dave LaRoche, and Kemer Brett were all pitchers in our high school league, and they mowed me down. I figured if I couldn't even get a hit against high school pitching, what future could I have in baseball? Of course, I didn't know at the time that all three of those guys would be in the big leagues battling players like Willie Mays and Henry Aaron not long after they disposed of me. Anyway, Rush and I hung up after deciding we'd try to grab dinner together if we ever happened to be in some city at the same time.

Not long after we spoke on the phone, Rush paid a visit to Sacramento that coincided with my Suns team playing the Kings there. The future mayor of Sacramento, Kevin Johnson, was our point guard. He had scheduled a major fundraiser for the inner-city school he had founded, St. Hope Academy. Rush agreed to attend the event with us and was so impressed with KJ's vision that he donated thousands of dollars to the school. At least three times more than anyone else gave. Kevin was grateful and gracious, but some of his progressive-to-the-core helpers went out of their way to show their disdain for Mr. Limbaugh, even as they processed the paperwork documenting his support of their cause—and their paycheck.

Rush was not surprised. He told me about when he once volunteered time on his radio program to help raise what likely would have been millions for a charity he was drawn to, the Pediatric AIDS Foundation. But his offer was rejected. They didn't want his money or national forum because they were afraid other supporters would object. He wanted to contribute to the fight against a horrible disease that afflicts innocent children, but the politics of the left viewed him as too big of a monster to be allowed to help.

I wonder what bothered them the most. Was it his belief that marriage, by definition, is an institution joining together a man and a woman? Was it his position that all people are created equal and have the right to liberty and justice under the law? Maybe they were scared by his belief that a smaller federal government and fewer restrictions on personal freedom were the best ideas. The Rush Limbaugh that I know is generous and decent, actually a shy person who comes alive in front of the golden EIB microphone, who pokes fun at some of the same insanities Mark Twain or Will Rogers would have targeted.

In 1997 my friend Steve Jones, former US Open Champion golfer, invited me to be his guest in Augusta to watch him compete in the Masters. Cindy and I had sponsored Steve for a brief time as he was getting started on the PGA Tour. We had also introduced him to his wife, Bonnie, during my first season of coaching at Southwestern College—the season I spent with Tim Fultz and the team I wanted to introduce Gary Payton and the SuperSonics to. Anyway, I invited Rush and Keith Erickson to join me. We had a blast trading off who slept on the floor of the small house Steve had rented. Steve got a bed every night since he was playing in the Masters. We thought that was the least we could do. Thanks to Steve, we had all-access passes for Tiger Woods' unforgettable first win at Augusta.

Rush and I hiked around the hallowed grounds, witnessing history from the first row. I'll never forget how gracious he was to the people who recognized him. Many not only spotted him but sought his advice. People wanted to pick his prodigious brain about things they might do to better their place in the world. Black people, mostly, if I dare say. They were asking the supposedly "racist" Rush Limbaugh questions and receiving fantastic advice about overcoming obstacles and never allowing oneself to make excuses or indulge in self-pity. In progressive circles, I guess that makes him a racist, but in real life, he came off very much like an encouraging professor.

Not long after our trip to the Masters, Rush returned the favor, and then some. "Hey, Paul, how'd you like to tee it up at Augusta National with me?"

How does one answer such a question?

"A lot," I think I said.

Jackson Stephens, president of the club, had invited Rush to bring a friend and enjoy a couple of perfect spring days as his guest. We arrived on a Friday afternoon and went straight to the course. We had time to play the magnificent nine-hole, par-three course before dinner, which we enjoyed in the Members' Dining Room.

There's not a golfer in the world who wouldn't have traded whatever they were doing those two days for what I was doing. The dinner, like everything else at Augusta National, was excellent in its simplicity. Understated perfection, but never ostentatious or opulent. "The way things oughta be," Rush might say. The beauty of the place is God-made and man-maintained. They don't nickel-and-dime the members or the patrons for food, either. I'm sure they make enough from the telecasts so they don't have to gouge anyone who gets hungry on the grounds, but that doesn't stop the folks at Disneyland, or airports, so I tip my hat to Augusta National.

Mr. Stephens was a fantastic host.

After dinner we went back to one of the "cabins" that borders the 10th fairway. There were four bedrooms downstairs, one in each corner of the structure. They shared a large living room with several sofas, tables, and chairs, comfortably positioned around the room which made for an inviting place for guests to gather to tell stories, drink, smoke, eat, play cards, or watch TV. Mr. Stephens' suite was upstairs. Around midnight, people started to turn in, so I asked Mr. Stephens what time we were scheduled to tee off in the morning.

"Wellll, Paauull," he drawled, "here's how we do it here. When you wake up, you tell George over there"—he nodded at George, who had been filling glasses and bowls for us since we came back from dinner—"what you'd like to eat, and he'll bring it to ya. The-en, head on down to the range and hit a few balls. When we're ready, we'll move over to the first tee and play us some golf."

Augusta National. Perfect spring Saturday. Great people. Almost nobody else on the course. I parred No. 12 on my way to an honest 84. That day was a little slice of heaven.

The future would hold many more fantastic times with Rush, like the time we went salmon fishing in Canada with Howard Slusher and Ken Hutcherson. After three days, everyone had pulled a nice salmon or two into the boat. Except Rush—and it drove him crazy. Finally, he got one on the line, but it missed going into the net on the first try. It was still hooked, so he reeled it out of the water again. Right before it was about to go into the net, a seal that had begun its dive from the opposite side of the boat sprung out of the water from under the boat and snatched his fish while it was inches from validating Rush's trip. Sadly, he returned fishless—with an undying hatred of all seals.

My endorsement of Rush seemed to fall on Aaron Goodwin's deaf ears, as far as I could tell. The vibe I got from him was if Rush Limbaugh was my friend, there must be something wrong with me. I'm not sure what Gary thought, but I was certain he wasn't going to become a "ditto head" anytime soon.

After the lockout ended, Gary Payton would be ready to play basketball. He was always ready. Grumpy or not, he was an amazing performer. He was a relentless, basketball-playing machine … always in shape, always more than competitive. He was combative! I wish the same could be said for the other projected pillar on which the franchise was built before I arrived, Vin Baker.

The first time I met with Vin, after the lockout, I found out that even though he and Charles Barkley both played power forward, there was nothing I could see in him that was anything like Charles. Or any other power forward I had known. Power forwards are the toughest guys in basketball. Generally, they are shorter than centers, but they often need to match up against them. So they must be more physical. Power forwards are the US Marines of the hardwood. They are generally the screen-setters, the rebounders, the men who don't mind doing the dirty work. I'd played with Paul Silas, Truck Robinson, Lonnie Shelton, and Maurice Lucas. And there were a couple of things I knew about power forwards. They don't make excuses. And they don't cry.

When I met with Vin in the locker room of the SuperSonics training facility, he was making excuses and crying. It was the first of countless times in our two years together. His alcoholism is now well-documented, but it was brand new in 1999. The lockout had done him in. He drank and partied himself into a forty-pound-overweight shell of his former self. In our meeting, he recalled through his tears the disastrous playoff defeat they had suffered the previous spring. He had been called upon to battle Shaquille O'Neal for much of the series, and it hadn't been pretty. Nobody blamed him, since nobody else could deal with Shaq that year, but he blamed himself. He felt like he had let the team down. Like he had embarrassed himself. While he wasn't admitting it to me that day in the locker room, his solution to his perceived failure had been to drink. A whole lot. He promised me he would never let his team down again. Promised we could count on him. He couldn't have been more wrong.

He started the season by missing eighteen consecutive free throws. One-eight. Eighteen! Try to miss eighteen in a row sometime. If you're trying to hit the rim, it's almost impossible to miss that many straight. That's how bad-off he was, following his extended summer of destruction. He never regained his All-Star form. By March 4, he got his free throw percentage up to 17 percent. Steve Springer of *The Los Angeles Times* sought out pop psychologist Dr. Joyce Brothers for a remedy. "I would ask him for a place where he's been when he felt warm, comfortable, and safe. A beach maybe. He should go to that place in his mind when he's about to shoot a free throw and not think about what he's doing."[3]

---

3 "Doc, Any Chance He Can Go Back to the Womb?" Los Angeles Times. Last modified March 4, 1999. https://www.latimes.com/archives/la-xpm-1999-mar-04-sp-13983-story.html.

That's why she got the big dough, I guess. To advise "Stop drinking!" wouldn't keep her and other shrinks in business very long. Simple advice doesn't create long-term customers. We have a friend whose wife is a psychologist. I once asked him if she ever cured anyone. "Hell no. Do you think she's crazy?" was his answer.

Bob George, author of the book *Classic Christianity*, once told me a story that involved a similar psychological prescription. He had a friend, let's call him Jim, who had always been a solid family man, who was a successful and respected businessman as well. A Christian man. Jim's son came to Bob one day with a troubling report concerning his father. "Bob, Dad is an inpatient at a psychology clinic. He just flipped out. It's like, suddenly, he can't handle reality. They've got him sitting in a room, hugging a big teddy bear. Will you please go see him?"

When Bob got to the clinic, he found Jim there just as his son had said, curled up with a giant teddy bear. "Jim, what are you doing hugging that bear?" was Bob's opener.

"Well, Bob, they told me that I need to get myself back to a time and place where I felt loved and secure. Back to when I was an infant, even the womb, if necessary. So they gave me this bear, hoping it would make it easier to get to that place."

"Oh, I see. So which is it, an affair, or are you stealing from your company?"

"Both," Jim admitted.

Vin Baker's situation was like Jim's. He didn't need to think about beaches or hug a bear. He'd been raised in a home where his father was a pastor. He sang in the choir, but now he was coming off a self-destructive summer. I think he knew he'd let down himself, his family, and God. He probably also suspected he'd ruined his career, but he was still years away from admitting and accepting any of this.

As it turns out, years later Vin would write a book about overcoming his alcohol addiction. In *God and Starbucks: An NBA Superstar's Journey Through Addiction and Recovery* (2017), he describes how hitting rock-bottom was a difficult, yet transformative experience that led him to renew his relationship with Christ and to embrace life. However, long before that, he was wreaking havoc on the court.

The SuperSonics in 2000 were a dysfunctional mess, despite our locker room having acquired a good "friend" of one of our star players. One day, one of them felt the need to throw a TV remote control device at the other one's head, so it was retaliation time when a nearby dumbbell was chucked back at the initiator's head. The SuperSonics' much-respected and beloved trainer, seventy-year-old Frank Furtado, stepped between them and caught a glancing blow on his head from the five-pound weight. The altercation was broken up, or so we thought.

One walked off while muttering, "I'm going to kill him." The other headed for his car with the stated intention of getting his gun. Two days later, they were hanging out like BFFs again, but even though they might have viewed the incident as a mere bump in their road together, those kinds of events leave a mark.

I decided I would try to tell the team about what basketball could be, if we could somehow rediscover our innocence. One of the people I hoped to reach was Vin Baker. He was the recent recipient of a new seven-year, $86 million-guaranteed contract. Knowing about his alcoholism, I had advised against signing him for more than a one-year deal. Owners Ginger and Barry Ackerley bought Aaron Goodwin's bluff, though, when he convinced them that Vin needed someone to believe in him to return to his All-Star form. He represented both Payton and Baker, and implied that the team would lose Gary if they didn't "treat Vin right." He bluffed them into believing some other team would be foolish enough to bet on a player in severe decline. The reality, of course, was that the contract only added to the pressure that Vin already had proven incapable of overcoming. Still, I was optimistic (or desperate or naive) enough to forego our usual pre-game film and X and O routine so I could share the story with them that this book was written to tell.

I couldn't include all the details that followed. I only had about a half hour to tell a very long story about how I got into coaching and the year I spent at Southwestern College. That's what I think I did that night in Denver. I told the abridged version of my Southwestern experience, and I had never told it better.

CHAPTER 7
NEGOTIATIONS, GOLF, AND DESTINY

My NBA playing career ended prematurely—at least, to my way of thinking. One of the reasons was because I was never very good at predicting how clauses in a contract would play out in real life. Negotiating points that seemed like we had "won" often brought out undesirable results when the smoke cleared. For example, after four straight All-NBA seasons with the Phoenix Suns, the team approached my lawyer/agent, Howard Slusher, about extending my contract. As I was entering the last year of the deal, still under thirty, I figured to be in a fantastic position to obtain a great contract. Howard was the best in the business, so all I needed to do was to sit back and let him do his job. But I had a "better" idea.

During our last negotiations four years earlier, Howard had pulled off a memorable piece of bargaining. Howard, Suns GM Jerry Colangelo, part-owner Larry Kartiganer, and I met for dinner in San Diego to finalize our five-year agreement. We enjoyed a nice meal. Then it was time to review it and sign.

Howard and I excused ourselves from the table and headed into the bar area so we could discuss our final approval. I figured it would be a short conversation. I knew the proposal came as close as any contract ever does to being what I hoped it would be.

"Are you good with this?" Howard asked.

"Of course. Let's go back to the table and sign it before they change their minds. This is great!"

"Yes, it's pretty much everything we asked for. Is there anything else you'd like?"

"Like what? This is awesome, Howard. Thanks so much for the fantastic job you did. I couldn't be happier."

"How would you like a new Mercedes?"

"I have an almost new 450SL"—$12,000 in 1975—"and an old Mercury that we bought from Alvan and Sara Adams. We'll probably trade that in for a new Mercedes. We can definitely afford one now!"

"No, Paul, I mean would you like it if I could get you a new Mercedes included in the deal? There's a way for us to structure this, so it hardly costs them anything. I think I can get them to throw one in."

"No way, Howard. If we go back in there and ask for something more, it might kill the deal."

"I don't think so. It can't hurt to ask. There's no way this would be a deal-breaker."

"Well, okay. That old Mercury is raggedy, but I can buy a car, so please be careful."

"Good," he said, "but I think we should ask for two Mercedes, now that I think about it. How'd you like two?"

"Are you crazy? No way they'd throw in two Mercedes-Benz. You've gone nuts. Frankly, Howard, I've been seeing signs of this for a while now. Let's forget about the cars and go back in and take the deal."

"Are you sure you wouldn't like two new Mercedes?"

"Who wouldn't? But then I'd have three. I don't want three cars, no matter how nice they are. But if you think you can pull this off, I'll give you the SL I'm driving now on top of your usual 60 percent."

We both knew Howard only charged by the hour and his fee never went above 3 percent in all the years he represented me. "Okay, but when did I agree to have my percentage cut to 60?" he fired back.

"Don't blow this, Howard!"

I admit I was nervous as we went back to the table.

"Fine. You can have the cars. Here's the pen. Let's sign this before Howard thinks of something else," they said.

Shortly after that evening, Cindy and I took possession of a new 450SEL and a 450SLC to go with it. And Howard had added a slightly used Mercedes Roadster to his garage. Apparently, Jerry and Larry had been concerned that because we took so long in the bar, we might be having second thoughts about signing. So when we came back, they agreed to add the cars. I was afraid we were being rude by taking so long and that we might be wrecking the deal by asking for something more, but that's not how it felt from the other side. Howard, Cindy, and I were now happy motorists. I didn't need the proof, but it sure solidified his status in my mind as the gold standard of sports attorneys. He did all but invent the profession, though, so his performance shouldn't have surprised anyone.

One would think I would have learned to listen to Howard after that night, but no. I think his biggest weakness was he listened to his clients too much. At least he listened to *me* too much.

When Mr. Colangelo opened negotiations with the intent of extending our original five-year contract with the Suns, I decided to go down a different road. Cindy and Howard didn't see it like I did, but I pushed for my vision anyway. I believed I was taking the high road by directing Howard to inform the Suns that it would be best for everyone if they traded me. John MacLeod was as fine a coach as the NBA had to offer, but over our five years together, it had become apparent that we had developed some irreconcilable differences. He didn't deserve to be fired, and I had too much respect for him and the organization to start down a "either he goes, or I go" path. Neither of us figured to start seeing eye-to-eye, so I concluded the only fair thing was to ask to be traded.

After many weeks of discussion, much of which became way too public (mostly my fault, I'm sorry to say), I was traded to Seattle for Dennis Johnson. Howard advised that it would be a perfect time to demand a new contract, since I was entering the final year of my commitment and had put together four straight All-NBA seasons. I, of course, thought I had a better idea.

It's a well-accepted practice to renegotiate in situations like mine, but I was reluctant to exert leverage when I, in fact, was not willing to sit out the season if they called my bluff. With a year left on the contract, I didn't believe I would be on the moral high ground by holding out. And I was eager to play. In fact, I might have paid them to let me play. I envisioned myself thriving in a backcourt alongside Gus Williams and "Downtown" Freddie Brown, protected by a frontline that included Jack Sikma, Lonnie Shelton, John Johnson, and Wally Walker.

I didn't plan on breaking my foot.

It happened nine games into the season. I had hardly missed a game in the previous eight years, but I couldn't ignore the growing pain in my right foot. The doctors figured out that I had a stress fracture of the fifth metatarsal bone, a diagnosis that very little was known about at the time. Bill Walton and I were two "pioneers" of stress fractures in the NBA, and the doctors flailed around, trying to figure out how best to proceed. Some prescribed rest. Some said surgery but couldn't agree on the proper procedure. Others said to suck it up because it was all in my head. Sometimes X-rays don't show the stress fractures until healing has begun, so they concluded there was no fracture. Except there was. SuperSonics' owner Sam Shulman said I was faking.

Mr. Shulman didn't share my naiveté regarding the purity of contracts and competition. Since Howard also represented Gus Williams, whose contract had expired, and who had decided to sit out until he was satisfied he was receiving a fair new deal, Sam acted as if my injury was a Slusher-orchestrated ruse to extort money from him.

For the first time in my life, someone had questioned my desire and motives for playing basketball! By taking the high road of not renegotiating when I had the leverage, I had handed Sam Schulman my weapon, which he then didn't hesitate to point right at my head. Since the SuperSonics would retain the "right of first refusal" after my contract expired, he felt he could extract revenge on Howard Slusher for keeping Gus Williams off the floor for an entire season.

"Holdout Howard" had crushed the SuperSonics on Gus' behalf. They caved completely. Howard not only more than made up for the missed salary Gus would have received for the year he sat out, but also added a new wrinkle to the "Mercedes kicker" he had used to my benefit with the Suns. He got a new Rolls-Royce thrown into Williams' new contract! But Sam Schulman wasn't going to let Howard win everything, so he decided to "go to the mattresses" in his negotiations with me. He put out the word throughout the League that the SuperSonics would match any offers, so there would be no reason for another team to waste their time signing me. Then he offered me a "make good," one game at a time contract. Second-round draft choices who never played in a single NBA game could get a guaranteed contract, but not me. It was a deal that would have netted me less than one-tenth of my probable market value. Basically, he was giving Howard the finger with my career. I had handed Mr. Schulman the hammer that he used to bash me in the head when I didn't take Howard's advice about renegotiating.

Howard, Cindy, and I all agreed to wait it out rather than accept Schulman's medicine. It looked like I would have to sit out the entire season if Howard couldn't find a way around what the SuperSonics believed was "checkmate." Half the season was gone by the time an opportunity for a jailbreak appeared. The San Diego Clippers were mired in a typical losing season. They needed an experienced guard, and since attendance

game-to-none margin in each of the rounds. More accurately, he replied, "Fo, fo, and fo."

Our team, led by Bernard King, played them right down to the wire every game. If we had defeated them, I truly believe we would have gone all the way. Alas, we were merely Moses' first "Fo."

As the season ended, I was named the NBA Comeback Player of the Year. One day later, I was waived, the victim of my brilliant negotiating acumen. When the Knicks tried to money-whip Kevin McHale away from the Celtics, Red Auerbach took it personally. New York made a huge offer to McHale to pry him away from Boston, but the Celtics exercised their right of first refusal and matched the offer. Then, Red Auerbach set out to make the Knicks pay for their sins. He offered every free agent on the Knicks roster at least double their market value, knowing New York could not stand losing almost half of their team. But I wasn't offered anything by the Celts, since my contract no longer contained the previously dreaded right of first refusal! So to remain fiscally responsible while saving face, the Knicks matched the outrageous contracts while they simultaneously waived me.

But at least, after six months of trying and failing to sell our house, the club bought it back, right? Of course, they did, being an honorable organization. And in a down real estate market, I felt good about it for a while. Not so much, though, a bit later. The New York market took a major upswing after we sold our house back to the Knicks, and they doubled their investment when they found a buyer a few months later!

Three years removed from forcing a trade out of town, my new road was leading back to the desert. Jerry Colangelo and John MacLeod wanted me back, and I wanted to come back. I couldn't command All-Star money anymore, but $300,000 per year was far from an insult. Jerry's only concern was that I was over thirty and had suffered some injuries since leaving Phoenix. "We need to have the second year protected against a career-threatening injury," Jerry requested. That seemed reasonable, even though defining something like that in a contract is not simple. Howard advised against this, but I thought I knew best. Still!

We agreed that we would arbitrarily pick a number of games that would be used to indicate whether or not I had suffered a career-threatening injury. We settled on sixty games, allowing me to miss twenty-two of the eighty-two and still have year two of the contract guaranteed.

"Jerry, this clause is designed to protect the club against injury, but what if I miss games through 'coach's decisions' or other circumstances beyond my control?" I asked.

"Paul, we both know the difference between a career-threatening injury and the sort of things you're bringing up. We understand each other. Trust me," Jerry replied.

No one has played a more influential role in my basketball life than Jerry Colangelo. He traded for me, traded me away, gave me opportunities to excel, released me as a player, and fired me as a coach. I'm sure I gave him plenty of headaches along the way as well. I didn't always like or agree with his decisions, but he always had the class to look me in the eye and explain his actions. He treated me with extreme generosity at contract time and, though a great businessman, he also valued integrity, family, and the love of the game in every move he made. Everyone in sports can learn much from the way he lives his life and conducts his business.

So imagine my surprise when, even though I had suffered nothing close to a "career-threatening" injury, unless one counts a sore hamstring that healed in time to appear in the last twenty-five games of the season (and playoffs) without any problems, the Suns refused to guarantee the second year. I had played in, you guessed it, fifty-nine games! Most due to the nagging hamstring that healed, but at least two were "coach's decisions."

Like Jerry, Coach MacLeod was a fine man who I respect greatly, but he must have felt and succumbed to the pressures of the Suns' ownership. They did not want to pay me for the second year of our deal, and that put John and Jerry in a tight spot. John remembered differently than I the conversation that had taken place between us when I had told him I could play against the Indiana Pacers if he needed me. I also missed two games because, even though I was day-to-day, they had placed me on the five-game disabled list. I was ready to go after missing three games. But I had to sit out two more due to the requirement to be out at least five games once on the list. Still, the arbitrator ruled against me. So my playing career ended. Too soon for my taste, but my playing days were over, nonetheless. So I set out to do what I had intended to do in the first place—coach.

All I needed was to find a team.

Cindy and I owned a house in Phoenix and another in La Jolla. NBA paychecks stopped, and we knew it was time to downsize. We prayed for wisdom to discern God's will in our lives. We believed the right move was to put both houses on the market and live in whichever one didn't sell. La Jolla has the best year-round weather in the world, and Phoenix had the best seven-month weather, coupled with five-month endless oven summers. I was rooting for the Phoenix house to sell first, but it was the La Jolla one that went.

We also prayed for a coaching job. I didn't think we were stretching God's capabilities, to tell the truth. I felt that I had unmatched experience, learning from a "who's who" list of basketball royalty. And I didn't wait for offers to pour in. I aggressively applied for coaching positions from coast-to-coast. We trusted God enough that we decided to accept the first job I was offered.

The silence was deafening. No jobs for me. Not even an assistant coaching position at my alma mater. Nothing. I had a year off in Phoenix coming up, so I decided I might as well take up golf.

I had never played much golf. Basketball, of course, plus volleyball and tennis, were the kind of sports I enjoyed. Quick, explosive games with a mixture of offense and defense. That's what I loved. But I knew my arthritic left knee was a ticking time bomb for those sports. I'd have to slow down, so why not get a start on the "old man's sport?"

Ping golf clubs were manufactured in Phoenix. Karsten Solheim was an engineer who also loved golf, so he messed around in his garage trying to create a better putter. He was so successful with making innovative putters that he decided to produce complete sets of clubs. To get the word out about his new company, he would send a representative to the Suns' practice gym at the Jewish Community Center on Maryland Avenue.

The Ping rep would hang around with our eccentric trainer Joe Proski in the closet-sized area where Joe taped and treated the Suns prior to practice. It consisted of an ice machine and a couple of tables—one for a player to sit on while Joe taped his ankles or treated something, and the other where players could sit and wait their turn. There was a cart that held tape and other supplies, a stainless-steel whirlpool tub on rollers, and a couple of folding chairs. It was the unlikely nerve center of the organization. Outside of Jerry Colangelo's office, it was the place to be for doing business.

Joe did the same work that it takes at least eleven people to do in today's NBA. He was the first person I ever knew who had his own T-shirts. "The

Prosk, Everybody's Main Man" was printed under a caricature of Joe. He passed them out to anyone who might help him increase his network for potential deals.

Today, a Head Athletic Trainer (which would have been Joe's title) has at least two assistants. The Dallas Mavericks, for example, also employ a full-time massage therapist. All teams have a strength and conditioning coach, who, in turn, has at least one assistant. Teams also employ a traveling secretary to make sure the flights and hotels are dealt with effectively. Joe did that before charter flights eliminated the need for assigning seats and changing planes in Chicago. He even assigned roommates, as antiquated as that is now. Every team has an equipment manager, who has an assistant to do the work. Three assistant coaches now sit on every bench, with several more behind, to keep stats, fouls, timeouts, and other notes. Joe did all of that. Nobody has to carry a projector and film these days, but back in the day, it was Joe's job to make sure they were always available at the coach's whim. Teams have psychologists on staff now, but there was no need for that with Joe around. Today, if a player needs a place to live, a good deal on furniture or a car, there is a "Community Relations" department. In Phoenix, all deals went through the Prosk. He only paid full price for gas and groceries, and it always bothered him that he couldn't find a way around that miserable fact.

If Joe had a connection, then Suns players did too. And Joe had a connection with Ping.

"Hey, Westy," I remember Joe saying while I was still a player. "If you want some free clubs, my guy here can hook you up with some Pings."

"Thanks, Joe, but I don't golf."

"Hey, Prosk," a new player interrupted. "Can I get some sound"— ultrasound treatment—"on my ankle?"

"Sure," Joe said. "Go put your foot on the radio. But don't change the station." Then, turning to me, he said, "But you might start playing someday. They're free."

"Yeah, but I'd feel bad having them waste clubs on me now. Thanks, anyway."

"Okay. Hey, Luke," he called to Maurice Lucas, our power forward who had grabbed twenty-five rebounds the night before. "Johnny Mac doesn't care about how many boards you got. You better get out of that tub and onto the court, or he'll fine your a—."

But now, a year after my playing days ended, I had time for golf, so I called Ping. Joe's guy remembered his offer, but things had changed. No more free stuff, but he would offer me a discount. I remembered former Major League catcher Bob Uecker telling how he found out that his world was different once his career ended. "I got to the clubhouse door, same as every day for many years. I nodded a 'hi' to the clubhouse guy, who then blocked the door and said, 'You can't go in there. Players only.'"

"Thanks," I said. I knew I couldn't golf without clubs, so I bought some Pings.

About eight years later, I was named head coach of the Suns. One of the perks of my new position was a deal to endorse Ping equipment in Arizona. Not that anyone would want to emulate my golf game, but I was Charles Barkley's coach, so I had visibility. I was back on the comp list with Ping, after a long and expensive absence.

One day, during the 1995 training camp, I arranged to fit in a round with two former teammates, Keith Erickson and Dennis Awtrey. Dennis happened to work for Ping at the time, and he volunteered to supply the fourth player for our group. We were pleased that he brought along Allan Solheim, Ping's president. But I must admit to some mixed emotions. Certainly not because Allan wasn't a great guy. He was. But I had a secret, and the president of Ping playing in our foursome would surely put a kink in my already-shaky game.

A few weeks before training camp, I had played some rounds with golf-lover and legendary rocker Alice Cooper. I first laid eyes on Alice the day he was baptized at Camelback Bible Church in Phoenix. He told about how he had rebelled against the teaching he had received from his parents, who had moved to Arizona when Vince Fournier (Alice's given name) was a child. They had moved so they could bring the Gospel to Native Americans in Arizona. But Coop wanted to go a different direction, so he moved to Hollywood as a teenager to become a rockstar.

He hung out at the Tropicana Motel in Hollywood with other hopeful future stars like the Chambers Brothers and Janis Joplin. Most shared a common bond in addition to a desire to become famous stars—Shep Gordon. According to Alice, he sought out Shep one day asking him to be his agent.

"I'll give it a try, Vince, but I don't know much about music," Shep said. "In fact, all I know is that whether it's Sinatra, Elvis, the Beatles, or most anybody else that makes it big, they all found a way to make the parents hate 'em."

"How about if I change my name to Alice Cooper?"

"I think that's the ticket."

After I witnessed Alice getting baptized, I knew his drug days were long past. We shared a few mutual friends, and I got his phone number from one of them and called him so we could arrange some golf.

"It's gonna feel weird calling a man Alice," I told Cindy.

"I think you should call him Vince," Cindy said. "I bet no one calls him Alice in real life."

"I know some people call him 'Coop,' but I've never heard Vince."

"I still say Vince, but maybe Coop. I could never call him Alice, though."

I dialed the number, and a woman answered. I assumed it was his wife, so I said, "Hi, Sheryl, this is Paul Westphal calling ..."

She interrupted, "Oh, hi! This isn't Sheryl, Paul, I'm Alice's mother. Just a moment, I'll get him."

After he came to the phone, Alice and I tried to get some golf on the calendar, but it was tougher than I expected to pin down a time. He kept suggesting afternoon times, but everyone knows that early in the morning is the only reasonable time to tee off in July.

"So, Alice"—if it was good enough for his mother, it was good enough for me—"are you still on rockstar time or something? What's wrong with mornings?"

"Ordinarily," he chuckled, "I like mornings in the summer better, too, Paul. But I'm tied up for the next couple of weeks teaching Vacation Bible School until after one."

Alice Cooper teaching VBS! Don't tell me God doesn't have a sense of humor. "Two o'clock at Camelback Tuesday sounds great!"

Before he started to endorse Callaway golf equipment, Alice had a line of "metal woods" that he was endorsing called "Alice Cooper's Heavy Metals." They had to decide between "Heavy Metals" and "Death Sticks." Close call. He let me hit a few shots with them, and I happened to hit some good ones. "Wow. I love these," I told him.

He said, "Keep 'em." And I was glad to. After all, my Pings were hooking and slicing up a storm. Maybe these would be what I needed to take my game to a new level. "Heavy Metals" were my best hope. Short of practice, that is.

I replaced my Ping woods in my Ping bag with my new Heavy Metals. But I covered them with Ping headcovers. No need to draw attention to my experiment. Besides, Alice didn't give me any Heavy Metals headcovers, if they even existed.

"Why are you teeing off with a 2-iron?"

It was a reasonable question Mr. Solheim asked as we began our round at Forest Highlands in Flagstaff. I didn't tell him it was because I didn't want him to see what was under my Ping headcovers, but I didn't lie, either.

"I haven't been hitting my woods too straight lately." That has been a true statement pretty much every day of my life, but it hasn't ever caused me to tee off with a 2-iron on a long par 4. I continued to hook and slice various irons off the tees, and hole No. 5 was no different. A par 5, I chose to slice my tee shot to the right, as did Keith, my cart mate and partner in our match. Dennis and Allan both hit down the left side, far from where our balls landed. Now was my chance! "Keith, I don't think they can see us. I'm gonna go for the green in two. I think I can blast it over the water with my three Heavy M.!"

Keith had seen me play. He knew I could only make the shot about one out of ten tries. Or if I chose to hit into the group ahead of us thinking I'd never reach them. "Let it rip, Paul. I'll watch out for the Ping guys."

"Nice, easy swing. Take dead aim. Smooth stroke, head still."

I told myself all the right stuff. My brain was the brain of a coach, but my body thought it was Superman. It tried to murder it with all its might. My Heavy Metal hit about three inches behind the ball, taking a spectacular gash out of the grass. The divot, the ball, and the club head all traveled about the same distance—ten or fifteen yards, I guess. All landed in the pond I was trying to blast over on the way to the green. I must have looked pathetic standing there, holding the broken shaft of my new Heavy Metal while Keith laughed hysterically.

By then, Allan and Dennis had hit their shots from across the fairway and gravitated toward Keith's laughter. They saw my posture and drove over to check out what was going on. Allan noticed the broken shaft in my hands. He thought one of his fantastic clubs had broken and wanted to investigate.

"The shaft broke, and the club head landed in the water. Unbelievable! I stink so bad at this game. Can I have a mulligan?"

Dennis and Allan answered in unison, "No."

My loyal partner leapt to my defense. "What do you mean, 'No?' You guys made an exploding club and then penalize our team for it? There must be a rule against club sabotage. You guys should be assessed a penalty. How do you sleep at night? Do your mothers know how low you are willing to go just to win a bet?"

I think Keith bringing Mrs. Solheim and Mrs. Awtrey into it was overkill. The next thing we knew, Allan was taking off his shoes and socks and rolling up his pants to above his knees.

"That's okay, Allan. Just leave it. I was just kidding about the mulligan. Let's play some golf!"

"No way," Keith instigated. "We want a mulligan." He laughed so hard he had to take a breath after every word. He knew what he was doing. Some partner, huh?

"I have to find out why our club head flew off! If it's bad construction, you get your mulligan," Allan said as he waded in.

I was reduced to hoping that the water would be too murky to find the evidence, while Keith continued his betrayal. "Take your time, Allan. There's nobody behind us."

Allan's determination paid off as he cried, "What is *this*?"

"Amazing! Somebody else must have broken a club here too. Incredible coincidence!" He knew I was kidding. He even smiled a bit. But I did not get my mulligan.

CHAPTER 8
ANSWERED PRAYER FOR A JOB

If I was that bad at golf in 1995, it's easy to imagine how badly I must have needed lessons when I retired from playing NBA basketball ten years earlier. My instructor, Paul Purtzer, was the first to realize (excluding Cindy, of course) that golf was not my future. Unbeknownst to me, he made a call to another of his hopeless golf students, Keith Province, and presented him with an idea.

Paul gave Keith my number. When I answered his call, he took a mysterious approach to reel me in. "Hi, Paul. You don't know me, but we share the same golf pro. Purtz suggested I call you because you are looking for a coaching job, and I have one for you!"

"Really? What job?"

"I'd like to tell you in person. Can we meet for lunch?"

I couldn't even weasel a hint out of him, so I agreed to meet him at El Chorro Lodge. Chicken-fried steak with chocolate icebox pie for dessert would hedge my bet if Keith's offer proved to be a waste of time.

After we had taken our place on the retro patio of one of my favorite spots in the Valley of the Sun, Keith started his pitch. "I want to offer you my job."

"What do you mean, 'your job'?"

"I mean, I'm the basketball coach at Southwestern Conservative Baptist Bible College, and I'd like for you to take over my position there. It doesn't pay enough for me to make a living, but the school's president won't let me quit unless I find a replacement. Preferably one who doesn't need to get paid. I can stay on as your assistant, if you like, as long as you don't mind if I'm not around much. I can help you get some players and attend some practices and most home games if I can fit it in around my work schedule."

"I've never heard of that school. Where is it?"

"Actually, it's only a few minutes from your house. 26th Street and Cactus Road."

"I've never seen a college there. Are you sure?"

"If you blink, you'll miss it, but I promise, it's there."

It was, too. Barely. There was a circular, gravel driveway that led past the slump-block dorms that housed up to maybe sixty students. Beyond the dorms was the two-story administration building, about 5,000 square feet of college, I figured. It housed the library, president's office, faculty offices, and classrooms. The only other structure on campus was a permanent "temporary" cafeteria that doubled as the headquarters of the Music Department. A couple of trailers were scattered to provide more flexibility. There was a gravel field with a backstop they called a softball field, where a few blades of grass could be detected trying to grow if they could only find some water. The desert was winning the battle of preventing the campus from being a livable bastion of higher learning.

Cindy and I had agreed we would accept the first coaching job I was offered. But this certainly couldn't qualify as a job, could it? Technically, paychecks should be associated with jobs, right? I decided to go ahead and agree to meet the president anyway.

Keith set up a meeting with Southwestern's president. We arrived in my little blue Mercedes convertible. I wasn't intending to turn heads. It was a modest car compared to the Rolls that my former Suns and Knicks teammate Truck Robinson drove around town. But turn heads, it did. The next best car in the parking area was probably an '84 Datsun. We rolled up to the Administration Office in a cloud of dust, parting a crowd of gawking students who had gathered around the building's entrance. Someone had tipped them off to our ETA.

Before we got out of the car, Keith explained that most of those who were gathered were members of the basketball team. They looked short. And White. I hadn't been part of a team that looked like that since my freshman year in high school. They reminded me of a suburban high school tennis team. Keith's explanation didn't make things much better. The ten young men waiting to check me out accounted for roughly one-fifth of the school's male population. Of the approximately 200 students, 150 were female. Not that there's anything wrong with that. This was a college that trained elementary school teachers and music ministry hopefuls. They had a highly acclaimed traveling singing chorale, "Chenaniah." And being selected for the group was the highest goal of most Southwestern students, male and female alike.

"Keith, do you mean to tell me that most of our team, should I accept this job, are musicians?"

"Pretty much."

Music and basketball is a difficult mix. In fact, Red Auerbach once warned me about it. When he first got the Celtics job, the team had a pretty good player named Tony Lavelli. It was in the days before the NBA really caught on in Boston. They used to play double-headers where a Celtics/Knicks game might be the preliminary event to a Harlem Globetrotters performance. Drawing a crowd often required some interesting promotional gimmicks. That's where Tony had come in, at least before Red arrived. As a popular accordion player, he was asked to entertain the crowd at halftime and after the game with his wonderful musical gift.

Red's first meeting with Tony started with a little flattery. "I hear great things about you, Lavelli. I'm told you're a real team guy. Is that right?"

"Yessir, Coach."

"If I were to ask you to do something for the team, would you do it?"

"Anything," Tony promised.

"Good. I'm really not sure you can do this, but I'd like you to at least try. I think it will really help the club."

"Just try me, Coach. I won't let you down!"

"Okay, Tony. Here's what I want you to do. I want you to take that accordion of yours and turn it sideways—then shove it up your a—."

Keith understood the story, having lived the frustration of coaching a team full of musicians. "Paul, that's a good story. Red was a wise man. I think if we tell the president that story, he might agree to provide a few basketball scholarships. But when you tell it, don't say 'a—'!"

One of the first things Southwestern's president did was tell me about all the rules the school imposed on students and faculty alike. Would I be willing to abide by them? I think we were both pondering that question. Since this was a Bible college, it didn't surprise me there would be expectations for certain standards of morality. After all, a prerequisite for students and faculty alike was a profession of faith in Jesus Christ as Lord and Savior. But "rules" and Christianity didn't necessarily mix. My study of God's Word brought me to agree with the Apostle Paul about rules. Humans just can't keep them perfectly, and perfection is the only thing God accepts.

Therefore, we all need to accept God's grace through repentance and faith in His perfect provision, Jesus, as the only way our sin can be blotted out of His sight. As Bob Dylan would say, "I pay in blood, but not my own."[4] Our changed nature, or becoming "born again," will then put a desire for obedience into our redeemed selves. Accepting Jesus' perfect sacrifice—not following rules—is what makes us Christians.

That's why I was pretty turned off when the president explained the rules. "No smoking, drinking, going to R-rated movies"—actually, attending movies in general was pretty darn questionable—"cursing, wearing provocative clothing, illegal drugs, sex outside of marriage, ungodly music, or gambling." There might have even been something in there about facial hair, I can't quite remember for sure. "Do you think you can enforce and abide by these, Paul?"

This is what I *thought:* "I don't smoke, but I'm not against it, except for the fact that it is unhealthy. I like cigars. They have C.S. Lewis books in their library. He smoked a pipe. They use sermons by Charles Spurgeon as texts. He smoked a cigar in the pulpit while he preached. Smoking is bad for a person, but so is overeating, and I don't see any rules against potluck dinners after church. I suppose I could live with the no-smoking rule. Jesus' first miracle was turning water into wine to keep the party going. And if it was grape juice, why did Paul have to tell the Corinthians that it's not okay to get drunk on communion wine? The Bible teaches not to be drunk, but never says don't drink. But I don't drink enough to miss it, so okay to the no-booze rule. Dancing? No problem for me to abstain from that, but didn't King David dance for joy? Oh well, dancing isn't my thing, but Tori (our ten-year-old daughter) is in Betty Johnson's Dance School. I think I won't ask if that's okay. Better to ask for forgiveness than permission, right? R-rated movies? Hmm. Does that mean no *Schindler's List* when they make it? I know there's a lot of garbage being cranked out in Hollywood, but one can really feel the pulse of a culture by watching movies. But I guess the kids ought to be studying anyway, and I can always watch TV. I wonder why there's no rule against that? I love what Dylan's going to say about that, 'Sometimes

---

4 "Pay in Blood | The Official Bob Dylan Site." The Official Bob Dylan Site. Accessed June 19, 2024. https://www.bobdylan.com/songs/pay-blood/.

you gotta do like Elvis did and shoot the damn thing out!"[5] Cursing? No problem. I always leave God out of my phrasing when I'm upset. But I did just quote the word 'damn.' That's not cursing, is it? I say it's not. Don't know if the president agrees, and I'm not asking. Cindy and I are true to each other, and we're married, and I think I'm fine concerning provocative clothing and illegal drugs. 'Ungodly music' might present a problem, depending on the definition. About all I listen to is Dylan or John Stewart, and I doubt many at Southwestern have heard of either. So okay on the music rules. And what is gambling, anyway? Is it playing the market? Betting five bucks with a friend on the golf course? Going for a steal in the backcourt? I could agree not to gamble stupidly, like refraining from buying a lottery ticket or trying to win somebody's rent money in a dice game, so I guess I'll take a chance and learn more about this job. I wonder if *that* is gambling?"

The president may have seemed like a caricature of a rule-following, straight-laced, sober-as-a-judge, circuit-riding preacher from another time, but he was no fool. This was a small, conservative college, existing in a cultural bubble, and really, what's wrong with that?

---

5 "Bob Dylan Quote: "It Will Scramble Your Head and Drag Your Brain About, Sometimes You Gotta Do Like Elvis Did and Shoot the Damn Thing Out …"." Inspirational Quotes on Beautiful Wallpapers - QuoteFancy. Accessed June 19, 2024. https://quotefancy.com/quote/950882/Bob-Dylan-It-will-scramble-your-head-and-drag-your-brain-about-sometimes-you-gotta-do.

CHAPTER 9
NEGOTIATING THE RULES

Even after I had decided I could live with the school's rules, I had a lot of questions. "Where are the games played? Where and when is practice? Is there a league of some kind? Who makes the schedule? What is the budget? Where does the money come from? How do they get to road games? Where do they stay? Are basketball scholarships going to be available? If I can find a basketball that belongs to the school, is there a pump?"

I started with an easy one, "How did the team do last year?"

"Pretty well. We won three games. Best season in several years."

Three and twenty, to be exact. I learned that home games were played at Desert Cove Middle School, a couple of blocks from the college. They were nice enough to rent their gym to Southwestern, but the renters had to sweep the floor and arrange the chairs before games. John Wooden still swept gym floors as UCLA coach because it set a humble example for his players. Also, he did it to find out if any of his players would notice their coach cleaning floors and decide to pitch in. I figured if Wooden could sweep floors, I could, too.

Practice was a different story. They didn't seem to put the same weight on practice that I expected to see in a serious program. "We usually practice down the street at Roadrunner Park a couple of times a week. We work around Chenaniah's schedule, so the times can vary," I was informed.

Roadrunner Park is *outdoors*! In the Phoenix desert, 100 degrees for twice weekly basketball practice? This couldn't be true. But that's how they rolled. And unless I could change things, they would be doomed to continuing as nothing more than an intramural program with uniforms (I didn't know yet that we would need uniforms, too!). Significant upgrades were needed to even approach ragtag intramural status. I would have to think of some way to improve the practice facility fiasco if I took the job.

"We are a part of the West Coast Christian Athletic Association along with Arizona College of the Bible, West Coast Christian College (located in Fresno), L.I.F.E. Bible College (Pasadena), Christ College (Irvine), and

Pacific Coast Christian College (Fullerton). We usually squeeze into a van or two for the trips to California and often sleep in sleeping bags on the floor of a church. Or sometimes someone might offer their guest bedroom. If you can raise additional money, you could rent a bus and stay in motels, but our budget can't do those things for basketball. It's not Chenaniah, you know."

I asked if there was some kind of national organization that might hold a championship tournament for the conference winners.

"Sure," he chuckled. "The 'National Little Christian Colleges of America,' I think it's called. We've never come close to qualifying, and it's held way across the country in Bristol, Tennessee. Either Christ College or West Coast Christian usually represents the conference."

The picture he painted for me was bleak. But I found it very honest as well. Keith and I did get him to agree to five "tuition-only" scholarships. They would not cost the school much. There were plenty of empty chairs in the classrooms. And it meant we could attract some needed local reinforcements to sit in some of them.

I was finished with my questions, but he had one for me. "I need to hear your Christian testimony before we can offer you the job, Paul."

I knew what he meant. Many people select "Christian" on their Facebook page, but it can mean many different things. Former President Barack Obama answered questions about his religion that way. So do Mitt Romney, the Pope, Oral Roberts, Donald Trump, most politicians running for office in a "blue state," people who attend church only on an occasional Christmas or Easter, and Unitarians who aren't even quite sure that there *is* a God, let alone a God whose only begotten Son rose from the grave. Many "Christians" don't think God created the world the way the Bible says He did. Many don't even believe the Bible is God's Word. And forget about miracles or prophecy. Lots of "Christians" make up their own belief system and call it Christianity.

But not at Southwestern Conservative Baptist Bible College. He wanted to hear me tell him about my conversion to "Biblical Christianity," which we Bible-believing Christians know is the one, true path to spending eternity with God. After all, that's what the Bible teaches, and the Bible is God's Word, backed up by confirmed prophecy fulfillment and historical and geographic accuracy that has been often dismissed, but never refuted.

If the Bible is not reliable, then God is a liar, and everything in the

Scriptures falls apart. "Eat, drink and be merry, for tomorrow we die."[6] That's what the Bible says is the next-best philosophy, the only sensible approach if God is removed from the equation. Skeptics might ask, "What makes the Bible so special? Doesn't it call for blind faith in things we can't know? Isn't one set of beliefs as good as another?" Reasonable questions, but a thorough study of creation, prophecy, and the resurrection shuts them all down.

Bob Dylan blows the billions-of-years-of-evolution theory away without breaking a sweat when he asks, "How many years must a mountain exist, before it is washed to the sea?"[7] If the earth had been here that long, erosion would have made the Himalayas lower than a politician's ethics. Or look at Israel. The Jewish people were scattered and persecuted for roughly two thousand years. Great civilizations tried to exterminate them. Still are trying. By a miracle unmatched in world history, they have returned to their homeland and thrived amid millions of people who surround them and work for the day that the Jewish people will be wiped off the face of the earth. And not only has all this happened, but the Holy Bible predicted it! Christianity is the only path that has its thesis validated by prophecy being fulfilled. And Israel, right there in everybody's face, screams this fact to a world that is increasingly dedicated to ignorance or worse.

And regarding the resurrection, I'm waiting for someone to disprove it. Anyone who honestly tries ends up becoming a true follower of Christ.

I gave Southwestern's president the short version of my "born-again" conversion. After all, faith in our Savior is not a complicated thing. Children can grasp the gift of God's love. I was a child when I accepted it. Probably six or seven years old. I had been taught the basics both at home and in Sunday School, but I still hadn't asked Jesus into my heart. But one day, I was outside playing "Cowboys and Indians." It's okay, my next-door neighbor was a real Indian (half-Hopi, half-Karuk), and I was an official Roy Rogers Deputy. I was hiding, waiting to "bushwhack" her before she could carry out her deadly intent directed toward me. She was smart and had never been known to attack where and when I expected her to strike. It was quiet—too quiet. My mind wandered to the things I had learned about sin. How we

6 1 Corinthians 15:32, paraphrased.

7 "Blowin' in the Wind | The Official Bob Dylan Site." The Official Bob Dylan Site. Accessed June 19, 2024. https://www.bobdylan.com/songs/blowin-wind/.

all are infected by it and how God desires that we give it over to Jesus, the Perfect Sacrifice, the Lamb who takes away the sin of the world. So that's what I did. Right there in the yard. I repented of my past, present, and future sins. My list of past and present sins wasn't very long, but I did know I had sinned enough that I fell short of perfection. I knew I could never be "good enough" to attain perfection on my own, so I joined up with the only One Who promised to take me to the place where *anyone* who accepts Him can live forever in His presence! Right after my "Amen," Caroline Dawn "Sissy" Numkena shot me with a rubber-tipped arrow. Right then was when I learned that God doesn't pass out "nothing-but-wins" to His children.

After sharing my conversion story, I was offered the job.

"What do you hope I can bring to the school?" I asked. "I'm such a strange fit here. Why me?"

"Paul, anybody can see that we need to add to and upgrade our facilities. We need a place for our students to assemble for convocations, concerts, lectures, even sports. We need more and better classrooms. We hope that you can help increase the visibility of our school, and God-willing, help us grow."

"I don't know how much I can help, but I will try to be a part of making your vision a reality. But I would like to ask you to promise me something too. What will it cost to fly to Bristol if we win the conference?"

"Probably about $5,000."

"Promise you will find a way to send us if we qualify—and you've got yourself a coach."

I never expected that this little place would ever see any nice, new buildings built. And he never thought for one second that we'd be winning a conference championship anytime soon. We both were secretly snickering at the other's naive hopefulness in the face of stark reality.

"Deal!" he smiled. And we shook hands.

CHAPTER 10
COLLEGE RECRUITING TIPS

Now what? Where do I start? One friend had an idea. "Why don't you put up a sign? 'If you like basketball, please come see Coach Westphal in room 205.'"

Finding talented players was a huge priority, but locating a place to practice and raising enough money to run the program were also vital components of the basketball puzzle.

A first-class health club had recently been built about five miles from campus. Ironically, given our Don Quixote-like quest, the club was named La Mancha. It had tennis courts, a pool, locker rooms, jacuzzis, weight-training equipment, an indoor track that encircled a beautiful basketball court, a restaurant, and anything else cutting-edge health clubs of the mid-1980s had to offer. I paid them a visit.

Being one of the most recognized people in town can be a pain when you slice a drive into someone's condo window, but when you're looking for a complimentary gym, it can really help. I told management what we were trying to accomplish, and they made their facilities available to us every weekday from two to five in the afternoon. We could have full use of the court, weights, and locker room. Free! All I needed to do was put in a good word for the club in some advertisements, and we wouldn't be a team with no place to practice anymore. "Hmmm, practicing outdoors at Roadrunner Park, or living like kings at La Mancha?" I pondered. "Maybe we should pray about it for a while." Well, not really. I jumped at it.

Having secured a place to practice, raising money and finding players to include in those practices remained large issues. Keith Province was staying true to his word. He had been finding some talented short guys who were looking for a place to keep playing basketball.

Recruiting to Southwestern would not be like it was when I was coming out of high school. And certainly not like it is now. These days, there are often layers of "advisors" and AAU coaches, along with the more traditional family members, friends, and high school coaches who might be involved in a player's college recruitment.

When I coached at Pepperdine, I saw some things that can best be described as fictional. Any program that is unwilling to bend some rules here and there has always been at a huge disadvantage. Even John Wooden drew a distinction between the "letter of the law" and the "spirit of the law." If a player is away from his family during a holiday, for example, helping to see he had a place to gather and eat should not be against any rule. And if it is, finding a way around the rule is not wrong, regardless of what the NCAA might decree.

I took a recruiting trip to Senegal while I was the Pepperdine Waves coach. The poverty was indescribable. Dakar is the home of Gorey Island, the gathering place where many enslaved Africans last set foot on African soil before they were loaded onto a slave ship bound for faraway lands. But I wasn't there to remove someone against his will. I was there to ask the permission of a proud Senegalese man to allow his son to voluntarily come to America—Malibu, at that—and receive a college education worth tens of thousands of dollars. I also offered his son the opportunity to pursue his talents on the basketball court. "Let him go with my blessing," I was told. "And thank you for giving my son this opportunity."

When Samba Fall arrived in Malibu, every rule had been followed to the letter. But now, there was a problem. He came with a paper bag that contained some underwear and little else. No clothes, no money, not even a toothbrush. The rules were specific about what we could give him. Nothing! So we put together a Nike duffel bag full of shoes and clothes that would fit, appropriate toiletries, and maybe even a little spending money. Then we threw it in the trash can. A minute later, Samba happened to pass by. He noticed someone had thrown away a perfectly good bag, and you can imagine how pleased he was when he retrieved it and found it contained many items that were just what he needed. I hope the statute of limitations has run out on our crime against the NCAA.

Contrast our violation to what we had to compete against. There was one junior college big man we were very interested in recruiting. Wyking Jones, one of my excellent assistant coaches, was told by the player's agent (I should say, "advisor," because players are not allowed to have an agent) that since we were not able to enter into a bidding war, we could forget about recruiting his player. Imagine our surprise when he ended up at another school in our conference!

But buying players has never been new in college basketball. That practice has been around as long as Kentucky has had horse racing. Cheating has become much more sophisticated than the traditional $100 handshakes or good grades for good play. As Charles Barkley put it, "I was a great student at Auburn—as long as I led the SEC in rebounding." What I learned about the evolution of the cheating that goes on is the stuff that would require a Rex Stout or Kinky Friedman to unravel in one of their mystery novels.

This is how one of the new scams works. A junior college coach, with the fictionalized name of "Dave," took over at a school desperate for a winning program. The school is in a very rough area, and the thinking was a winning team could help provide some much-needed positive energy to the institution. Dave laid the groundwork of his operation by forging strong bonds with a few key tenured teachers. Dave's best players would be signed up in classes where their presence would never be required. They would pass these classes if they did everything Dave told them to do. You see, Dave's specialty is second chances. His scheme fills a need, because there are many players who can play basketball very well yet have no business or interest in being a college student. He took players who failed at previous schools. Maybe they had a drug problem, or a run-in with the law. Usually, they had bad SAT scores and horrible grades. But they all had game and were down to their last chance.

Dave gave them that. He promised these desperate young men that they would become eligible for a scholarship at a four-year school if they would follow his rules. He would make sure their academic credentials became acceptable for the next level if, and only if, they played well and would agree to attend the school of Dave's choice. He would be the auctioneer, parceling his players out to the highest bidder. Schools needed players, players needed schools, and Dave needed money. The system was stacked against them, he rationalized, so why should a lack of academic prowess be allowed to keep a kid from living his dreams?

There were a few problems to overcome, though. For example, what if a player didn't want to go to the school to which Dave sold him? In that event, Dave gummed up the gears by having one of his professors withhold a key grade, claiming that a project hadn't yet been completed (which was true, since the player hadn't done any projects). Once the player "saw the light" about which school should be the college of his dreams, the professor would "find" the lost project and submit whatever grade was needed to qualify.

Still, Dave had a problem concerning how best to "wet his beak." Cash in a paper bag is so Nixonian. It might do in a pinch, but he had developed much more sophisticated ways. In lieu of cash, he once tried to solicit an honorary doctorate degree from one university. His best-known scheme was to become a promoter of college basketball tournaments. This is how it might work. He would send Johnny to Cheating State Teachers College, Mohammad to Internal Revenue Tech, Jamal to Gamblingtown University, and the best player, six-foot, eight-inch power forward Malique "Bad Mofo" Mofou, to the University of Tex-Mex at New Mexico.

Typically, the host school would pay visiting teams anywhere from $10,000 to $50,000 to participate in their "Holiday Classic." This is a good way for college coaches to schedule wins. Home games are always a boon to a team's chances of victory, and even more so when one can select inferior opponents. Unbalanced scheduling is one of the major flaws in the DNA of college basketball. At least in the NBA, every team plays forty-one at home and forty-one on the road, against the same competition as everyone else. But a high major university often plays a preseason schedule of ten home games and maybe a neutral-court tournament. In Hawaii, if possible. An 11–2 record is about the worst result a decent team should expect. The 11–2 start can be followed by playing .500 ball in the balanced conference season and a meaningless conference tournament to yield twenty-plus wins virtually every year. Twenty wins keeps coaches from getting fired, and provides a ticket to the lucrative NCAA March Madness cash bonanza. Paying for some early season wins is a good investment.

The less-wealthy schools are happy to take the appearance fees and a chance to upset a larger college. It even happens sometimes, but when it does, the giant killer can be certain they will never be invited back. Nobody likes a guest who doesn't know his place.

Where others see a stacked deck, Dave envisions a chance to become a dealer. By becoming a promoter, his cashflow could look legitimate, as well as cause money to run into his wallet from several directions. Kind of like how many times the IRS taxes the same dollar. Whether you earn it, spend it, invest it, or die with it in your pocket, the IRS gets a piece every time. In

Dave's scam, he might ask Tex-Mex State to pay him $40,000 to "promote" their "Classic." His "expenses" for placing CSTC, IRT and GU might add up to $10,000 per school. Thirty thousand for Dave, promised players to schools, wins and home games for Tex-Mex, upset opportunities and road trips for the smaller schools. Who loses? Multiply this scam a few times over, and it's easy to see how Dave can afford to make the payments on the apartment building he owns where his players can live for a very affordable, government-subsidized rate—if they stay in line.

The desperate young men who fall in line with the "Daves" of basketball often don't come from stable home lives with much positive parental guidance. Very much unlike my situation when I was entering college. I not only was not looking for a handout, but I also didn't want to attend any school that cheated. I figured if it did, and got caught, the probation would hurt me as much as the guilty parties, so I made it known to all recruiters that I was looking for a school that followed the rules. And I wanted to stay in Los Angeles.

At first, UCLA seemed like the place for me. But Jim Hefner had other ideas. He was Bob Boyd's relentless assistant, and he made it his mission in life to get me to enroll at USC. He assured me they ran a clean program, and I would be safe from any kind of career-damaging probation that dirty programs are prone to receive. He admitted that he couldn't vouch for the football program, but he did maintain that star player O.J. Simpson actually had a legal job with real responsibilities. I found out later what it was. Simpson's job was to make sure no one stole the Los Angeles Memorial Coliseum, the home of Trojan Football. Evidently, he did a magnificent job, as it remains standing at the very same location to this day.

"No problem," was Coach Jim "Little Jimmy" Hefner's favorite expression.

"Coach, is it true that SC has plans to build a basketball arena that's even better than UCLA's Pauley Pavilion soon?"

"No problem, Paul. I expect it will be finished before you graduate." Maybe he thought it would take me a while to graduate, but the new, "better than Pauley" Galen Center did get built. So what if it took almost forty years?

"Coach, if I come to SC, I'm a bit worried about the beds in the dorms. There's only about six feet of space between the wall and the closet. I don't think there's any way for those rooms to accommodate someone who's 6'4'."

"No problem, Paul. Don't worry about it."

"Okay, but I have another concern. At some of the other schools, they have parking for athletes right by the gym. Does SC have that too?"

"No problem, Paul."

Great, I thought. But when I arrived at school, my dorm bed was just like everyone else's, and there was no parking near the gym without a permit. Remembering Coach Hefner's recruiting pitch, I sought him out.

"No problem, Paul! This is what you need to do. Sleep diagonally and bend your knees. Also, you can take $50 down to the Student Union and buy a parking pass for the semester that will allow you to park in the lot next to Bovard Field. Anything else I can do to help, don't hesitate to ask."

From then on, Coach Hefner was "Little Jimmy," at least when he wasn't around. But the years have reduced my pain, and now I appreciate the difficulties Coach Hefner needed to overcome. I truly am in his debt. I thought I knew everything, but in truth, I was so naive and sheltered that there was only so much I could grasp about the way things were. Years later Little Jimmy and I were able to laugh about those USC days. We were both so young.

CHAPTER 11
THE VALUE OF HIGHER EDUCATION

I've always had mixed emotions about the value of college. Still do. On one hand, it's great for future doctors and dentists. Even lawyers, I suppose. But too many people go to college just to pass four or five years in some kind of pre-maturity party limbo. Let's face it, how many more film students and sociologists does the world need?

My father never went to college. After he graduated from high school, he needed money, so he worked. He took engineering classes at night, which allowed him to gain enough knowledge and skill to earn a living as an aeronautical engineer until he retired. Old-school, but effective.

When I was at USC, you could always find the football players either at practice, the cafeteria, or playing pool in the basement of Marks Tower. Stars, like O.J. Simpson I was told, didn't accept a scholarship because then he wouldn't be allowed to hold a job under NCAA rules. Instead, he had his job guarding the Coliseum. It kept his income flowing, so he could afford to pay for his own tuition. And room and board. Transportation and clothing too. Nice work if you can get it.

Basketball players never rated that level of status at USC, but I do recall a memorable conversation one of my teammates once had with one of our teachers. He had skipped class for three-and-a-half weeks. When he dropped back in, I heard him ask the professor, "I didn't miss anything, did I?"

At another school, I once heard one of my players get asked if he had written and submitted his term paper yet. "I don't know."

Still another unforgettable quote from a scholar-athlete I knew happened when a truancy-prone individual was spied attending and participating in a ceramics class. When complimented on his newfound academic excellence (okay, attendance), the player smiled, "That class is just me and a few ladies making plates. Not bad."

Personally, even though I graduated in four years, I thought college was a waste of time. Not totally, because I did take away a few useful lessons. I started out intending to be a business major. Then, I took economics. I never missed a class, took notes, did all the reading, studied, and got help from a tutor. I did everything I could to prepare for the first midterm exam. When I sat to take the test, I wrote my name on the paper, and stared at it for about ten minutes. Then, I got up and headed straight to the registrar's office so I could drop the class and change my major. That test might as well have been written in Chinese for all I could make of it. Now, of course, I don't feel as dumb as I did then. I realize nobody understood economics, and those who passed the course are the same people who have been messing up our economy for all these years. If only P.J. O'Rourke's book, *Eat the Rich*,[8] had been written and used as the economics textbook of my generation ... the world would be a much better place. That's for sure.

Religion class was a joke too. The professor didn't even believe the Bible, yet he thought he knew more than God. And Spanish class, mandatory for graduation, was little more than teaching us how to order from Taco Bell.

Kinesiology, taught by Dr. Gene Logan, was a great class. Dr. Howard Slusher's one-unit health class was one of the toughest and best classes I ever took, even though he only gave me a "B." I have no idea why it was called "Health 101," because it was more like a pre-law class. Howard was a truly great teacher before he became a truly great sports attorney, right before he became a truly great executive at Nike. I'll never forget one of the legal lessons he taught his health class.

"There were two identical cases involving chicken franchises versus chicken franchisees. Identical. Kentucky Fried Chicken prevailed in their case, while the now defunct franchise, Chicken Delight, lost. Why?" Dr. Slusher posited.

"Were the cases really identical?" one student asked.

"Yes."

"How can that be?" we asked and gave up.

Like Socrates, he answered our question with a question, "Have you ever tasted Chicken Delight's food?"

Apparently, the judge liked KFC. Chicken Delight was just too greasy.

So despite my mixed experiences in higher education, I could see that

---

8 O'Rourke, P. J. *Eat the Rich: A Treatise on Economics*. New York: Open Road + Grove/Atlantic, 2007.

Southwestern College had a purpose for existing. Their courses were geared to training future missionaries, youth pastors, music ministers, and Bible teachers. Not a ceramics class in sight.

My early days in Redondo Beach with Coach Nick Comitas.
I'm in the middle of the front row.

My dad made this backyard hoop where countless games were played
on our driveway under the Westphal Athletic Code.

From my Aviaton High School playing days.

Me between two great men, my dad and my high school coach, Ken Brown.

Me with USC Coach Bob Boyd and teammates Mo Layton, Ron Riley, and Joe Mackey.

Forced to practice using my left hand growing up came in handy.

I never went anywhere without a basketball.

NBA first-round draft pick making up my own rehab routine using my bride's makeup case during our honeymoon. Things are different now.

With the great Red Auerbach celebrating our 1974 NBA Championship.

Visiting with John Havlicek during the 3-on-3
competition in Las Vegas one summer.

To put on a Celtics uniform after
graduating USC was a dream
come true.

Being traded from the Celtics to the Suns opened up my future in basketball.

I always tell the kids, "Practice your free throws!"

1985-86 Southwestern College Eagles.
Back Row: Me, Glenn Strutz, Mark Sonmor, Justin Cawood, Danny Coyle, Tim Fultz, Gene Denning, Wayne Jones, Marvin Temple, Keith Province. *Front Row*: Jeff Nimtz, Brett Foudray, Bob Shaeffer, Theo Skwarzynski, Dave Narloch, Walt Rock, Dan Deruiter

On the road with my Southwestern Eagles.

Celebrating winning our conference that sent us to the
National Little College Athletic Association tourney in Bristol, Tennessee.

The Southwestern team, after learning of Coach Westphal's brain cancer diagnosis,
came to our backyard in 2020 (despite COVID-19) to have one final reunion.

Coaching these Suns players with such diverse personalities was a beautiful thing to behold. Falling short of the championship in 1993 continues to leave a knot in my stomach.

Chuck is one of a kind. Bigger than life in basketball with a huge heart for people.

Coaching these Sonics players, another group of diverse personalities. While there were those who were true pros, it only takes a few with their own agendas to drag their team down.

Me with four wise men, basketball legend Coach John Wooden,
Pastor Ken Hutcherson, Keith Erickson, and Larry Elder.

With Buffy & John Stewart,
the evening they changed the
"De-fense" chant to "Be-Friends."

Leave it to my wife to capture a photo of me having that
memorable conversation with Coach Hubie Brown.

The Gaither Vocal Band (Michael English, Wes Hampton, David Phelps,
and Bill Gaither), Doug Anderson, and me when they sang the National Anthem
before an Indiana Pacers playoff game.

With the great Bill Russell.

With Jerry Colangelo. With gratitude. I owe so much to this man for bringing me to Phoenix.

I met Mike Lupica and Bob Ryan during my rookie year: two knowledgeable, excellent, and trusted members of the sports media who remained that way throughout their careers.

With Howard Slusher. He was my college professor, then my NBA attorney/agent. Most of all my friend, like a protective big brother.

On the golf course with Ken Hutcherson, Rush Limbaugh, and Howard Slusher.

I was blessed to be mentored by Coach Cotton Fitzsimmons.

With Lionel Hollins. I couldn't be more grateful to this man and all we've been through together.

Long past our Suns playing days, getting together for lunch with my former teammate, Alvan Adams and trainer Joe Proski. These men are two of the best!

With the brilliant basketball teacher Pete Carril.

The night I was inducted into the Naismith
Memorial Basketball Hall of Fame.
Incredbly humbled.

My granddaughter's view of her grandpa
getting inducted into the HOF.

Three generations of Westphals: My dad "Pappy,"
son Michael, and me.

Fun with my toddler girl, Tori.

With Cindy, Michael, and Tori at
the beach one of our many summers
escaping the Phoenix heat.

Taking my grandchildren, Kai and Maile, to
a Suns game. It's true when they say, "If I had
known how wonderful it would be to have
grandchildren, I'd have had them first."

CHAPTER 12
SHAMU

My sometimes-assistant coach, Keith Province's, first recruiting target for Southwestern was Danny Coyle, a lightning quick five-foot, ten-inch point guard who had just graduated from Arcadia High School in Phoenix. His father, Terry, was one of the most respected coaches in Arizona. Danny had the game for a higher level of college ball than we could offer, but he happened to be dyslexic, which limited his academic opportunities. To describe him as a player, I steal a line from bluegrass legend Rodney Dillard. Danny was "slicker than deer guts on a doorknob." But because of his dyslexia, asking him to function as a typical point guard was not going to happen. If I diagrammed a play, he would nod, and then proceed to the opposite side of the floor from where the little "x" on the diagram indicated he should be. It's not a good thing if your point guard doesn't start the play from the correct side of the floor, but he was too good a player to put on the bench. I would have to adjust.

This was my first coaching job, and the decision I made to accommodate Danny Coyle would serve me well in the future. Instead of asking him to do something that was contrary to his wiring, I just told him to take what he saw, and then we installed a system where everyone else would adjust to where he started and what he did next. I didn't know it at the time, but I was learning how to coach Charles Barkley.

My friend, Rob Yardley, once said to me, "In a lot of ways, coaching Charles Barkley must be a lot like coaching Shamu"—SeaWorld's famous killer whale.

"What do you mean?"

"I have a friend who helps train the dolphins at SeaWorld. When they do a trick right, they get a fish. If they don't do it right, no fish. It's amazing what they learn to do with this method. When Shamu arrived, the same teaching techniques were employed. The only difference was, because of his size, he got lots of fish. Shamu was a great student at first. He did tricks and ate fish. But then he stopped doing tricks, so they withheld the fish.

Shamu didn't decide to start doing tricks when that happened. Instead, he decided to trash the tank. Two hundred thousand dollars' worth of damage because he didn't like his trainers keeping his fish. So SeaWorld instituted the 'Shamu Rules'—if Shamu does a trick, he gets fish. If Shamu doesn't do a trick, he gets fish."

"I don't think your analogy holds up, Rob," I said.

"Really? Why not?"

"I don't think Chuck likes fish."

A good team can have one "Shamu." Maybe it even needs one. But it can't survive two. Once A.C. Green tried to leave the "dolphin tank" to swim with the whales, and even though A.C. was known for his professionalism and work ethic, I had to put him back with the other dolphins.

Barkley was a practice-killer. Much like Bill Russell, he was so much better than even most All-Star level players that he had to hold back to keep from dominating a practice to the point of ruining it. And when he reeled back, he held back too much. His boredom and clowning around would wreck the session if he wasn't challenged. It was a genuine problem, and I dealt with it by holding him out of practice as much as possible.

Day-of-the-game shoot-arounds were especially problematic for Charles. First, he was not a morning person. Second, our walk-throughs were a time for literally walking through how we planned to defend certain plays, doing some film work, and participating in shooting practice. Maybe some two-on-two or individual work for younger players who needed extra conditioning, but we didn't require strenuous exertion from any of our players who figured to play the most in the game that night.

Not being a morning person, Charles did tend to push his star privileges further than I preferred. While the other fellows were always ready to go in their practice gear, often, he would show up in sweats and Timberland boots. At least they had rubber soles. And since all he was expected to do was watch tape, shoot some free throws, and walk through our defensive rotations, I chose not to make it an issue.

But to a player like Green, it was an abomination. Nobody practiced harder than he did. He was always early, always working up a good lather, and always committed to the ideal that nobody would ever outwork him. He *was* a morning person, since he had no known vices. Except maybe a little "Charles-envy." Because it did bother him to see Chuck get the Shamu treatment. Nobody could blame him. I didn't.

A.C. Green had been brought to the Suns as a free agent to counterbalance Charles. And hopefully have some of his work ethic and self-control rub off on him too. Since Barkley was near the end of a long-term contract and Green arrived with a brand-new five-year deal, he would make more than twice as much money as Charles during his first season with the team. It would change soon, but it still bothered Charles. And it bothered him even more because he sensed A.C. seemed to think that because of his professionalism, he was worth more than Charles.

"Look at this stat sheet," Barkley said to a gathering of reporters after a game. His locker was close to Green's, and there was no way A.C. could miss what was being said. "There are two interesting lines here. One guy had five rebounds and seven points. This other guy had nineteen and thirty-six. Guess which one is making $7 million this year?"

A.C. Green would not be human if things like that didn't bother him, and one day he had had enough. So when our morning shoot-around arrived, he decided to make a Charles-like entrance one minute before practice. At 8:59 a.m., he burst into the gym wearing his practice uniform and flip-flops. It was very funny. Even Charles laughed. Especially Charles. Not only because he can take a joke, but also because that happened to be a day that he had arrived early for practice, sneakers tied and ready to work. So when I blew the whistle and announced, "Today, we're going to change up our normal routine. Let's start out with some full court running drills," watching A.C. Green participate in the five-man weave wearing flip-flops was one of the funniest things I've ever seen. I did feel bad for him, though. After all, it wasn't his fault that he made more than Chuck. And he was justified in being hurt by the way Charles had drawn attention to it. But still—a team can't have two Shamus.

PICK-AND-ROLL

Charles was, after Shaquille O'Neal, the worst pick-and-roll defender in the NBA. Maybe ever. One of the biggest factors in our game preparation was to figure out how we could hide Charles' deficiencies versus the various angles and options we might see from our opponent's pick-and-roll attack. We had at least five different defensive schemes, but it was a constant struggle to get Charles on the same page as his teammates.

One day, as we were beginning our morning practice in preparation to play against Jerry Sloan's Utah Jazz and the awesome splendor of the Stockton and Malone pick-and-roll, I remembered Danny Coyle. Instead of watching Charles mess up one situation after another, I'd let him do his thing and ask his teammates to adjust!

"Chuck, we've tried everything so far this season to defend the pick-and-roll. Stockton and Malone are going to kill us tonight if we don't figure this out. All our schemes can work, but only if we're all on the same page. So, how do *you* want to play this tonight? Push it baseline? Fine. Switch it? I'm okay with switching. Help KJ through? That can work. Double it early? Bring Mark across the lane early and leave Ostertag open at the basket"—actually, that was a high-percentage strategy. He only caught about half of the passes that were directed toward him. And if he did catch one, he only completed half of his layups. Twenty-five percent efficiency is good defense!—"Chuck, I don't care. Just tell us how you want to play it, and that's what we'll commit to doing."

"Coach, tell Kevin to let him try to split it, and I'll clothesline John's neck as he goes past. They won't run it anymore after that!"

I *think* he was kidding, but I had to admit, the clothesline strategy had the best chance of success. With Charles, there was always a fine line between genius and lunacy.

"Let's try something that won't get you fined and suspended, okay? Please pick an option from our playbook."

"Let's force it baseline," Charles decided.

"Okay, tonight we push the side pick-and-roll baseline."

The first time the Jazz ran the side pick-and-roll that night, everybody played it perfectly. Except Charles. Kevin Johnson forced Stockton toward the baseline, where Barkley was supposed to be waiting. But Charles was up on Malone's shoulder, ready to "show" on the screen. Stockton walked in for an uncontested layup.

"Time-out!" The team gathered around me. "Chuck, you said to force it base! KJ did it, but you were up!"

"My bad. Sorry. Let's play it another way. I'll show and help him through from now on."

Next time they ran it, KJ forced Stockton toward the screen, where Charles was going to be showing to slow Stockton down enough for Kevin to get through and catch up. Only Charles wasn't showing. He was back by the baseline, where he should have been the first time. This resulted in a wide open fifteen-footer for one of the best shooters who ever lived.

"Time-out! Chuck?"

"My bad," sounding sincere, he muttered, "let's just double it from now on."

When we tried to double it, Chuck messed up again. Everything we tried, he screwed up. He did enough good things in other ways that the game was right down to the wire. Predictably, they ran a side pick-and-roll in crunch time. Charles jumped out on Stockton, stole the ball and proceeded down the floor for a breakaway dunk. Game, set, match. Suns win!

After the game, most of the players had showered and filed out. I had about a dozen people in my office, various reporters and friends sitting around enjoying a tough win. As he was leaving, Charles stuck his head in first, then entered. "Hey, Coach, how'd you like the way I played the pick-and-roll tonight?"

"I've gotta admit, I was a little worried about you tonight. But I guess that's why we put up with all your crap. You came through when you had to."

Playing to the crowd in my office, he announced as he strutted out, "I *can* play defense, I just don't."

Anyone who saw *Forget Paris* must be wondering how we ever got Charles to perfectly execute the play that opened the movie. In the film, I diagrammed a play that was designed to give Charles a shot to win the game as the buzzer sounded. People might rightly ask, "If Charles couldn't follow directions, how did he execute that play so flawlessly?"

Easy. They filmed the action first, and *then* taped me diagramming the play. I had the luxury of watching it on film, and then drawing it up for the scene exactly as it would appear. It was the only time Chuck was truly coachable, and it was all a Hollywood trick.

Danny Coyle wasn't Charles Barkley. Nobody was or ever could be. But for our little team at Southwestern, it was worth it to adjust to his idiosyncrasies. He was the perfect point guard for us, and in signing him up, Keith gave us a chance to beat American Indian Bible College and Arizona Auto. We'd need more, though, if we hoped to compete with our hated crosstown rivals, Arizona College of the Bible.

CHAPTER 13
FILLING IN THE ROSTER

With the point guard position taken care of, Keith and I decided to go for some experience. Well, at least age. Walt Rock had attended Southwestern a few years previous, where he and his wonderful wife, Michele, had met. After they got married and started having babies, Byron and Eric, Walt quit school and concentrated on earning a living.

When Keith ran him down, he was a six-foot, two-inch, twenty-four-year-old bus driver for Phoenix Country Day School. According to Keith's calculations, Walt had a year of eligibility remaining. And since the "Little Christian Colleges of America" didn't have any rules refuting this analysis, we proceeded on that assumption. At 6'2", Walt would be our power forward.

And he wouldn't be the worst power forward I'd ever coached, that's for sure. Not that I'm bitter, but if every power forward/center I coached had Walt Rock's heart, brain, and attitude, if not his body—I believe at least two of my times being fired would have been greatly delayed. During my time as an assistant in Dallas and head coach in Phoenix, I was privileged to witness up close and personal two of the greatest power forwards ever in their primes. Dirk Nowitzki and Charles Barkley—wow! The flip side of those two was Baker and Cousins. They could, and did, bring a man to his knees. If there had only been a way to put Walt into those all-pro caliber bodies. He was as professional in his approach as any person with whom I've had the privilege to share a locker room. I knew with Walt Rock as our team's power forward, our squad would never back down from any challenge. He would be our team's backbone.

He would also be a great recruiter. He had a friend from the "muni leagues," another mid-twenties married father of two. Dan DeReuiter had never played college ball. He was a six-footer, maybe, and ball-handling was not his thing. He was a shooter. Not a passer, not a defender, not a rebounder. A shooter. And more importantly, he was a maker! Dan had deep range and a quick, if unorthodox, release.

Dan worked the graveyard shift at Mayflower Moving Company to support his family. He and his wife, Kathy, had two little mouths to feed with more to come. No one could understand how Dan could commit to working all night and then attend classes in the mornings and basketball practice every afternoon. "When do you sleep?" he was often asked.

"Stoplights and class," was his sleepy reply. I do not know how he and Walt did it. Even more remarkably, how did Kathy and Michele do it?

The commitment shown by the DeReuiters and Rocks reminds me of a story I heard Coach Abe Lemons tell concerning how soft we Americans have become. The NCAA had been agonizing over a proposal that would allow first-year students to participate in varsity basketball without spending a year on the freshman team first. Even Lew Alcindor had to play freshman ball at UCLA the year his group thumped the Bruin varsity in their annual scrimmage. Oh, the varsity went on to win the NCAA title that year, even though they couldn't beat their own freshmen. No question that the future Kareem Abdul-Jabbar was ready to head straight to the NBA, and definitely to the varsity. But the conventional wisdom said that youngsters needed that first year to adjust to college life.

Notre Dame Coach Digger Phelps spoke for the status quo at a meeting of NCAA coaches, going on (and on) about the importance of "matriculating" the tender youngsters into the rigors of the academic, social, physical, and emotional challenges of major college athletic competition. Finally, Abe could stand it no longer. "Excuse me, gentlemen, but may I please say something? I do understand the great concern out there about the many pressures facing our youngsters as they 'matriculate.' I know when I was seventeen, crawling through the mud, on my belly in Korea, during the times I was ducking the bullets that were flying over my head, that that's exactly what was going through my mind. 'How in the hell will I be able to matriculate at a university if I have to deal with the pressure of going to class *and* playing varsity intercollegiate basketball at the same time?'"

Needless to say, soon after Abe's speech, they started allowing freshman eligibility in the colleges and universities of our nation. Many youngsters went on to prove they could be tougher than conventional wisdom had maintained. But I believe even Abe Lemons would have thrown a salute toward Dan and Walt. It might not be dodging bullets in Korea, but what they did was heroic in its own right.

Some of our returning players also had time challenges. Bob Nedimeyer and his wife had children and bills to pay, yet he tried to remain committed to the team as well. As a full-time husband, father, and student, he had managed to pull it off during Southwestern's three-win season the year before. The one with twice-weekly, optional outdoor practices. But with the new schedule, he would have a difficult time juggling everything, so he spent the season appearing at games and practices as his schedule would allow. It was agonizing for him. He had played quite a bit the year before, but now he was being asked to spend more time and energy yet play less. It would be tough for anyone to accept, and Bob handled it as well as possible. Sometimes he needed to step away for a week or two, but then he would come back to the team. Then leave again. Then return. He wanted to contribute, but his priorities were too demanding and real for him to be able to justify participation with such a diminished role.

Mark Sonmor was another holdover. He was a serious student and member of Chenaniah. He liked basketball, but he loved his other activities. Even though he had been one of the best players on the previous year's team, his prospects for major playing time diminished with each recruit. To his credit, he stuck it out despite the hit his personal hopes would take. Still, he could only be a part-time participant in practices, which led to less playing time. He passed the character test of going from starter to little-used-reserve gracefully. It could not have been painless or easy.

Wayne "Basketball" Jones also was a singer who was a returning player. Even though he couldn't make it to all the practices, he proved to be a person we could count on as someone who had a love for the game and always brought an enthusiastic attitude. Additionally, I will always remember Wayne as the worst "faller" I have ever seen. Most people know how to roll, or at least cushion their landing in some way, when the inevitable basketball spills take place. Not "Basketball" Jones, though. If he went down, he seemed to land face-first every time. Splat! Either his face, or some other hard edge of his body would spring a leak. It was amazing in its splendid tragedy, but he would always get up with a smile as he limped off the floor in search of medical attention.

There were at least two other potential returning players who had the ability to be starters on our squad, but they did not feel they could afford to dedicate themselves to the new time commitment. Keith, our master recruiter, would have to beat the bushes a little harder.

I'm still not quite sure where he found Dave "Looch" Narloch. I think he saw him playing at Roadrunner Park one day. Dave was a motorcycle guy. Tall (if you call 6-foot-3-inches tall), lanky, and inexperienced. He was the kind of kid who could fall between the cracks. Quiet and kindly. There one day, gone the next, leaving people wondering, "What ever happened to Dave?"

We called him "Looch" because the guy behind the microphone who introduced the lineups before our first game mispronounced his name. Phonetically, it's "Nar-lock," with the "h" sounding like "k." But when Dave was introduced as "Dave Narlooch," what else could we do but start calling him "Looch?" We had no choice.

Looch was the only player on the team who could jump well enough to dunk in a game situation. I'm sure that with some training he could have high-jumped close to seven feet. We even had a lob play for him. And though it only worked about one out of four times, just having the play and knowing that we had a dunker on our team gave our guys some swagger. He started every game at small forward. He kept a slight grin on his face and hardly said a word all season. He went to class, played hard, and averaged about seven points and five boards per game. The perfect complement to our final recruit, Jeff Nimtz.

Nimtz became our six-foot, one-inch starting center. If he had played football, he would have been a linebacker on defense and a running quarterback who could throw when needed on offense. He was the best passer, defender, and rebounder on our team. He had the skill to play guard, but his mentality was basically "trenches." A few years later, I would coach Dan Majerle. Jeff and "Thunder Dan" had similar mentalities. I hated to *ever* remove either from the court. They didn't need rest and loved combat. They wanted to guard the toughest opponent, and more importantly, they could!

The season we drafted Majerle to the Suns, I knew he would succeed, in part, because I had seen Jeff Nimtz succeed. Not that the level of competition or their talent were comparable. Of course, they weren't. But both had the combination of talent, a combative nature, and *heart*.

DAN THE MAN

When a person has those attributes, success follows. Dan was our second first-round selection, taken 14th, seven slots after we chose Tim Perry of Temple University.

Tim enjoyed a nice career in the NBA, and Suns' fans will ever-esteem him because he was one of the three starters we traded for Charles Barkley. One night after everyone else in the Suns offices had gone home, Jerry Colangelo and I brainstormed about finding a way to make a deal work that we had been trying to consummate for Charles. The Philadelphia 76ers insisted on receiving three starters in return for their eccentric superstar. We'd already agreed to give them Tim Perry and Andrew Lang, our starting center. But they demanded either Majerle, Kevin Johnson, or Jeff Hornacek. Including any of those excellent and popular players in the trade deal was a tough pill to swallow. The Sixers were adamant. Draft choices would not get it done. If we didn't include one of our prized guards, there could be no deal.

"Let's give them Jeff," I blurted. We all loved "Horny," truly one of the best shooters ever to pass through the NBA. And a great citizen, fan-favorite, and fixture in the Valley of the Sun. "If that's what it takes to get Barkley, we can't not do it."

Jerry didn't say a word. He picked up the phone and told Philly we'd do it for Perry, Lang, and Hornacek. Just like that.

Back to Majerle, though. If you timed them one at a time with a stopwatch, Tim's time was faster than Dan's. But if they raced, Dan would win!

When we drafted a phenomenally gifted athlete who played Dan's position, things got interesting. This draft choice tore up the Los Angeles Summer League, averaging about twenty-five points per game that were punctuated by several highlight-quality dunks. People compared his athletic gifts to Michael Jordan's, but instead of being flattered, he got carried away. He expressed sentiments that indicated his own unique talents would take him to different heights. At least, that's how Dan read it.

Dan decided to see for himself. And his opponent soon found out there was a big difference between summer league and an NBA training camp. One day near the end of the first week of camp, I arrived at the gym early. He sat by himself, head down, troubled about something. I went over to him, put my hand on his shoulder, and quietly asked, "You okay?"

"My dreams have been crushed."

"It's only the first week. Hang in there. Things'll get better."

"No, they won't."

"Why not? What do you mean?"

"Majerle."

That was all he said, and quite honestly, all that needed to be said. Every drill, every scrimmage, Dan had taken it upon himself to guard him closer than Donald Trump guards his tax returns. Every time he turned around, Thunder Dan was there. If he tried to cut across the lane, he would be stood straight up by a forearm to his chest. When he inhaled, he smelled Majerle's breath. Dan didn't punk him in a classless, unsportsmanlike way. No trash-talking or blows designed to injure. He "out-combatted" him on such a monumental level that he was left with no confidence. It was gone, never to return.

Just as Walt Rock could have been a great NBA power forward due to his mentality and professionalism (all he lacked was a body that could compete), Jeff could have been another Dan Majerle with a bit more size, strength, and quickness. But he sure had enough to play center for us at Southwestern.

THE STARTING LINEUP

Finally, we had gathered all our starters. Coyle and DeReuiter in the backcourt, Narloch, Rock, and Nimtz up front—5'9", 5'11", 6'3", 6'2", and 6'1". College basketball, here we come! Of course, John Wooden won his first NCAA Championship with a pair of six-foot, one-inch guards and a front line measuring 6'3", 6'5", and 6'5", so height isn't everything. At least, that's what coaches try to make their teams (and themselves) believe when stuck with a short team. But even with our starters in place, we needed to fill in with a few more players, if only to be sure we'd have enough bodies for practice. Especially with the unreliable schedules Sonmor, Nedimyer, and Jones needed to keep.

Fortunately, Bret Foudray and Eugene Denning were able to enroll without the need of a scholarship. Both had played high school ball the year before, and at 6'2" and 5'10" respectively, they would be able to fill in capably to give us a lift off the bench wherever one might be needed. Bret possessed a nice mid-range jumper and a good knowledge of the game. He was versatile enough to fill in at any of the front court spots, and Gene was the perfect complement to relieve either Dan or Danny. He was one of those fearless, game-changing types of guys who could put his stamp on the game immediately. Sometimes bad, but mostly in a positive way. He reminded me of Bill Sweek, a "fasten-your-seatbelts" kind of player who helped UCLA win some titles in the Alcindor years.

As enrollment closed and classes began, we had our team pretty much in place. Five starters on scholarship, two key subs, a soccer player from Costa Rica, and a few semi-present singers. We also had room for any miscellaneous students who might like to sign up, like Glen Strutz (at about five-feet, two-inches, diminutive even by Southwestern standards) or Justin Cawood. Justin didn't have a basketball background, but he was very likable and had a good sense of humor. And he wasn't in Chenaniah!

We had a team, a place to practice, and some fundraising ideas that should make it possible to have uniforms, pay officials, get to our games, and even occasionally have enough money that we'd be able to eat. But there was at least one thing I hadn't figured out yet—transportation to and from practice. The La Mancha gym was about five miles from campus, and most of the guys with cars were not heading back toward campus after practice. Their jobs and homes were in the opposite direction. I drove a two-seater, so I could give one player a ride. Another could go on Narloch's motorcycle, but it was obvious we had a transportation problem. This wasn't SEC football, after all. Even the managers get Escalades there. No, our guys were destined to be hitchhikers or pedestrians if I didn't think of something.

Pastor Larry Fultz tells the story of a conversation that took place around the Fultz family dinner table in 1985.

"How was school today, Tim?"

"Great. Coach wants me on the basketball team!"

"They have coaches for intramurals? Wow, they didn't have that when I was in college."

"No, Dad, not intramurals. The varsity!"

"Tim, you never even played in high school. You're five-feet, eleven-inches and about 140. Surely you've gotten something wrong."

"Nope. Coach Westphal said he needs me."

"Why don't you take this story from the beginning, okay?"

"Sure. He saw me drive up and waited for me to get out of my car"—a

'70s-something Chevy Nova he had bought for $48 that barely ran. "He asked, 'Are you a student here?' After I told him yes, he wanted to know if the Nova was my car. He seemed real interested in me. Then he asked if I was in Chenaniah. When I told him no, he told me that he had an idea to help me get to know some fellow students, even though I don't sing. He suggested that I could make a lot of new friends driving three or four guys to and from practice. In fact, he made me promise I would. 'You're just what we need on our team,' he said!"

It's true. I told Tim all he needed to do was drive four other players to practice every day and he would be a full-fledged college basketball player. When he agreed, it solved our practice transportation problem. Now we needed to raise some money.

CHAPTER 14
FUNDING THE EAGLES

Keith Province said that one of the greatest things Southwestern College had going for it was the cheerleaders. He wasn't kidding. Those young ladies were mostly from church-going homes, and all were serious about their Christianity. They were, without exception, wholesome, sweet, and talented.

They were cute and modest, even though they thought the school's policy, which called for the cheerleaders' skirts to be at least mid-knee length, was too old-fashioned and restrictive. But they didn't rebel. Before every game, they sang an acapella version of the "Star-Spangled Banner" that was as beautifully harmonized as any I'd ever heard. The Isaacs could top the girls' version, but I don't think they'd been formed in 1986, so as far as I can verify, the Southwestern cheerleaders' version was the world's best at the time. Keith suggested we find a way to involve the girls in our fundraising efforts.

"If we can incentivize the girls by telling them they can go on a California road trip if they reach a certain goal, I'll bet they would raise a ton of money," he said.

For some reason—Willie Mays and my natural contrarianism, I guess—I grew up as a San Francisco Giants fan despite being from Los Angeles. Still, I thought the Dodgers had the best-looking warm-up jackets in the world. Our Southwestern school colors were blue and white. Because we were the college's only sports team, and we hadn't bought uniforms yet, we could make our colors anything we wanted. And I liked blue and white. From there, Keith and I hatched the fundraising scheme.

"I know someone who can make us some Dodgers look-alike warm-up jackets that read 'Southwestern' across the front. Then, we can get that basketball-dunking eagle logo that Larry Toschick created for us embroidered on the back." Larry was a world-renowned wildlife artist, and my parents' next-door neighbor in Pine, Arizona, who had designed a fantastic-looking logo to replace the wimpiest-looking eagle in the world that had served as our previous school mascot. "Fifty bucks is all it will cost us if we order at least a hundred. If we can sell them all for $100 each, we can clear $10,000 by selling two hundred! Ten thousand bucks should get us off the church floors and into some cheap motels, with enough left over for 'training table' (donuts and burgers) on road trips. Let's promise the girls that anyone who sells at least ten jackets can travel with the Eagles to California."

"Bonnie Buckingham will probably sell a hundred all by herself," Keith predicted.

He wasn't far from right. Bonnie and the rest sold over 150 jackets, and the players found enough friends and family members to hit up, that we realized our goal. I think I helped move a few items myself, even though I had to give one away to prime the pump.

I had met New York radio and TV personality Don Imus a few years earlier while playing for the Knicks. Again, it was one of my closest friends, Mike Lupica, who introduced me to an icon. I arranged for a ticket that allowed Don to sit with Mike when the Lakers came to New York. After spending five minutes with him, I could tell he could be bought. As one of the highest-paid radio personalities in the country, and a thrifty one at that, Imus could buy anything he chose. But he was a creature of radio, and that meant he loved "payola." Not criminal, scandal-type payola, but free stuff was the key to his controversial, but golden heart. With that knowledge, I sent him a complimentary jacket. It had a red "VH-1" featured right underneath the diagonally scrolled "Southwestern." I included a note that told him about our team, hoping his mention of their availability might cause a few Imus fans to lend their support.

His *Imus in the Morning* radio show had led to the new VH1 network hiring him to become one of America's first video disc jockeys. Cable was just exploding onto the scene, and MTV and VH1 were vying for control of a promising, but uncharted music video market. And he adopted Southwestern as his favorite team, wearing his free jacket on the air and touting our progress every week!

"My friend, Paul Westphal, the former Knick and NBA All-Star, is coaching my new favorite team—the Southwestern Conservative Baptist Bible College Eagles. These guys play for the love of the game. They are what college basketball is supposed to be all about. We crushed Arizona Auto last week, and this week, we play American Indian Bible College. We're gonna kill those guys, getting ready for our showdown against those weasels from Arizona College of the Bible. Now, you fellas on the team—we're going to show a Madonna video right now. Don't watch this. It'll be over in three minutes, and then you can come back, and we'll talk about our playoff chances."

I'm glad Southwestern's president didn't have cable.

ALL ABOUT THE SHOES

Selling jackets wasn't the only form of support we received. Howard Slusher agreed to donate his entire commission for negotiating my contract with the college. Okay, 40 percent of nothing is nothing, but he did arrange for Nike to provide some free shoes. To our guys, that was a very big deal. In fact, I wasn't too far-removed from the early days of the still raging "shoe wars" myself. I remember the days before free shoes for players were taken for granted.

At USC, we wore Chuck Taylor canvas Converse shoes. High or low tops, black or white. Those were our choices, even though all we could choose were white high tops because Coach Boyd wouldn't let us wear black and was afraid we might sprain our ankles with low tops. Adidas had just entered the American market, but Coach Boyd was friends with Joe Dean, the Converse representative, so we wore Converse. I would get blisters bigger than a silver dollar on the bottom of my feet and dime-sized sores on my toes. I had to wear three pairs of socks and use Vaseline, baby powder, and moleskin to protect my feet from those foot-killers. Chuck Taylors were worse than misspelled tattoos.

When I got to the NBA, there was Converse, Adidas, PRO-Keds, and Puma to choose from. Nobody got paid, but if you wore a company's shoes in a game, a player could usually score another free pair or two. That was how it was until Nike came along. Maybe a handful of star players had some kind of minimal endorsement deal, usually requiring them to conduct a few clinics in exchange for $100 and some free shoes. But Phil Knight and Nike arrived with a new strategy. Not wanting to rely on buying ads like the other companies did (probably because his upstart company couldn't afford to do so), he decided to pay the athletes for wearing his shoes. He figured that even though a company might be able to buy an ad on the back of a magazine such as *Sports Illustrated*, the cover wasn't for sale. But what people saw on the cover was authentic, and that's what people wanted to buy. Since he couldn't buy an advertisement on the cover, he bought the feet of those who would appear on covers. That's how marketing history gets made.

By 1976, my fourth year in the League, my feet were unattached to any commercial commitments. I wore what anyone gave me, willing to try anything that had a good grip on the floor if they didn't tear up my feet. Our Suns team was playing in the Western Conference Finals against Rick Barry's Golden State Warriors. As we were getting off the bus at our hotel after practice, Alvan Adams told me some guy from some new shoe company had invited us to his room. "This guy has a trunk full of sneakers. Called 'Nike,' I think. He says he'll make custom shoes to fit our feet and pay us $1,000 to wear them!"

We'd have played in huaraches for a thousand bucks, and not too long after that meeting in the Oakland hotel room, Alvan and I were Nike men through and through. Over the years, my relationship with Nike grew. Phil Knight and I were occasional tennis partners, and as the company grew, so did the paychecks. As well as the quality of the shoes, which is their passion at Nike. Once, when the unheard of at the time sum of $1 million was thrown around, it was proposed to me that I pull a "Pele." That is, would I, Paul Westphal, consider legally changing my name to—"Nike"? That way, every time I scored, the crowd would hear the announcer say, "Nike for two!" Honestly, it was discussed. Possibly, even seriously, but eventually dismissed. It was a cool idea, but I didn't have the guts to "Just do it." And neither did they.

As Nike grew, though, so did my compensation from them. At the peak of my career, Howard negotiated a six-figure deal that was groundbreaking at the time. After Howard, Phil, and the late Rob Strasser finished negotiating that contract, Howard had a bit of time to kill before his flight.

"You want to grab a beer or a bite to eat, Howard?" Phil asked.

"Okay, but what I want to do is squeeze another five thousand bucks out of you guys." Howard being Howard. And squeeze it out, he did. After they put him on the plane, Knight told Strasser, "We have to hire that guy. He's the best negotiator I've ever seen." So they did, and years later, Howard was still with them. He made sure the Eagles had new Nikes, and no group of players ever appreciated them more.

CHAPTER 15

RED, NO—PISTOL, YES.
IT'S ALL GOOD

"Simply selling jackets isn't going to get the job done," Cindy said. "It's a good start, but you'll need more. Why not hold a golf tournament?"

"Who are you and what have you done with my wife?" I asked the woman who, just recently, had reminded me, "God, family, job, golf—pick three." The same three I told her when I married her, only golf had somehow sneaked in there. Golfers understand.

"This isn't about golf," she said. "Maybe the time you spent golfing last year wasn't for nothing after all. Surely you met a lot of people in the golf world who can help you do this right. Plus, you know retired ballplayers who would love to come to Phoenix in the winter and play golf for free. If you add it all up, it spells golf tournament."

"If you add something up, the answer can't be a phrase," I teased. "It has to be a number."

"You know what I mean. I think you should go for it."

My first call was to Red Auerbach. Even though Red had once said that "golf is not a sport, it's a trick," I was sure he would love to help out a former Celtic who was trying to join the ranks of his disciples to enter coaching. Bill Sharman, Bob Cousy, Bill Russell, Tommy Heinsohn, Don Chaney, Dave Cowens, Paul Silas, Don Nelson, and K.C. Jones, to name a few. I was sure Coach Auerbach would want to extend the helping hand he must have used many times before. After I spelled out my request for his presence, Red didn't hesitate to respond. "Hell no. I'm not gonna fly across the country for a stupid golf tournament. I'm too old for that sh—. And I hate golf."

RED BEING RED

What might sound abrupt in Red's answer didn't bother me. That was just his way. Years later, Mike Lupica would provide an example of an interaction between Red and Mike's dad, Bene Lupica.

"How's your dad doing, Mike?" I had asked. He had recently turned eighty, and I knew he had suffered a fall.

"He went to a doctor who told him he should use his cane so he could avoid hurting himself badly in another fall. Of course, he ignored the advice. We backed up the doctor's prescription, but he stayed stubborn and refused to use the cane. The Old Man (Mike's name for Red) asked about Pop while I was interviewing him, and I told him about the cane impasse. Red snorted, 'Gimme his number.' Even though they had never met, Red called him. When my pop answered the phone, Red got straight to the point. 'Don't be a schmuck!'

"'What? Who is this?'

"'You know who it is.' He did too. 'Stop being a schmuck and use the cane.'

"Red Auerbach, instrument of compassion. From then on, Pop used his cane."

When former Celtics get together, they can tell Auerbach stories all day long. Phil Jackson might have surpassed most of his coaching records, but to me, Red is still the greatest non-playing figure in NBA history.

His negotiating prowess was masterful. He hated agents. And before they became more inevitable than crooked politicians, he swore he would never deal with one. He predicted they would ruin sports, and who can say he was wrong? Pragmatist that he was, he did negotiate my contract with Howard Slusher—but only because I asked him if he would work out the contract with my "friend, Howard, who also happens to be an attorney." Red agreed, but the answer surely would have been "no" if I had called Howard my "agent."

Cindy saw how Red treated agents in the early days of their NBA existence. Prior to a playoff game in Washington, he was sitting with friends at a round table in the Capital Center restaurant. Larry Fleischer, attorney and agent, was the head of the NBA Players Association and one of the first and greatest agents to impact the League. Red hated Larry because Fleischer had the temerity to represent Don Chaney, probably the best defensive perimeter player in basketball and an underpaid starter for the Celtics. When Red refused to negotiate with Fleischer on Chaney's behalf, Larry signed Don to a deal with the ABA's Spirits of St. Louis. What else could he do? But Red never forgave him. So when Mr. Fleischer arrived at the restaurant and was seated a couple of tables away (but directly in Red's line of sight), Auerbach stood, squatting as he lifted his chair to baby-step his way into turning a 180-degree maneuver that accomplished his goal. He wouldn't have to gaze on Mr. Fleischer's face as he sat with his friends, even though he had turned his back on those at his table as well!

After Chaney's defection, Red did agree to deal with agents. Just because he hated them didn't mean he could continue to deny the reality of their existence. They had been elevated to "necessary evil" status. Just like referees.

Cheerleaders were a different story. Red always maintained that the *game* should be the thing. Not entertainment. The game itself, if properly appreciated, could provide all the entertainment basketball lovers should ever want. Nobody hated the pyrotechnics, gyrating dancing girls, and loud music-filled circus atmosphere that routinely defines the in-arena NBA experience more than Arnold Auerbach. "Showtime" was the opposite of what Red loved about the game. He appreciated substance, not the Hollywood perversion that had crept eastward from the land of the hated Lakers. Red swore the Celtics would never have dancing girls as long as he had breath.

Finally, the marketers in the Celtic organization gained enough strength to declare that the Boston Celtics would at long last join the rest of the League by adding dancing girls at the games in the season to come, no matter what Red Auerbach thought. Much like the children of Israel had acted when they chose to disobey Moses and God by erecting and worshipping the golden calf after they decided that they knew best, the marketing geniuses decided to do it their way. And like Moses, Red didn't take it the way they hoped. He passed away before the dancing girl season began. He never did have to endure a Boston Celtic home game polluted by creeping Laker-ism.

Our golf tournament fundraiser would need to proceed without Red's help. No hard feelings. But Celtic great Sam Jones did attend. So did Truck Robinson, Keith Erickson, and the great Elgin Baylor. Growing up in Los Angeles during the Baylor-West years, I had been dubbed by *Times* sportswriter John Hall, "Jerry West Jr." Flattering, for sure, but too much typecasting for my taste. Even though my size and race suggested it would be West, my real role model was Elgin. Howard arranged for several of his football clients to be there, including Franco Harris, Sam "Bam" Cunningham, Mike Haynes, and Dan Fouts. Future US Open champion Steve Jones represented the golf world, and Pistol Pete Maravich agreed to be our guest of honor. Red or no Red, it was an amazing turnout for our little school's event. Maravich joined us for golf, spoke at the banquet, and gave a private clinic for our team. He golfed about as poorly as I did, but he spoke like the next Billy Graham.

Pete and I were close to the same age. He was a senior at LSU when I was a sophomore at USC. We traveled to the bayou to play them during the 1969–70 season. We found out later that Coach Boyd had been warned about starting too many Black players in that game. He ignored the threat, and we knocked off the Tigers 102–99. I held the Pistol to fifty. And to think people have always said I couldn't play defense. I guess I showed them that night, huh?

Actually, for a man who is the answer to a great trivia question ("Name the top three single season scoring average leaders in NCAA men's basketball"), keeping him at fifty wasn't so bad. That's what I tell myself. Since Pete averaged over forty-four points each of his three seasons at LSU, I'm not exactly the only one he lit up.

I have never played against anyone who worked harder to get his shot than Maravich. The most attempts I ever had in a college game was twenty, thirty in the pros. Pete regularly hoisted over forty shots, often, more than fifty! The energy required to get that many attempts in the air, especially when the other team's defense is set to prevent those shots, is staggering. He never stopped sprinting around screens. A back screen here, a double screen there. Unlimited range (even before the three-point line was invented), creativity, energy, opportunity and a license to shoot. Someone will break Joe DiMaggio's fifty-six-game hit streak before anyone averages forty-four points, three years in a row again.

When he spoke at our dinner, he gave the message that he lived the last five years of his life. He would go anywhere he was asked, especially to speak to youngsters. He hoped someone would pay his expenses, which we did, but if someone didn't offer, he still would go and pay his own way. He felt God had let him live so he could tell about how Jesus had changed his life. He cared about little else, and if he had to pay his own way to spread the good news of Jesus Christ, so what?

People hung on every word. He told of his childhood, encouraged by his parents to prove that a White man could dominate in basketball. I don't believe that Pete had a racist bone in his body, but the society where he was raised certainly did. He was single-minded and relentless in his desire to earn a scholarship to college and then make millions. He was born to fulfill these goals. During the day he was never without a basketball, even in class. At night, he would lay on his back in bed, practicing the backspin and follow through on his shot release, as he shot the ball perfectly toward the ceiling. He told how his father once had him lean out the window from the back seat of their car and dribble down the road as he changed speeds to make it challenging. Pete said it wasn't too bad except when the road shoulder was gravel. When that happened, occasionally, he'd catch a pebble in the head. That would make him concentrate even more, just like when he practiced his dribbling in the mud during thunderstorms. Pete figured if he could handle the ball under those kinds of extreme conditions, a couple of defenders and a full court press would be nothing.

He became a national celebrity at LSU, and beer and women entered his life in a big way. Even though he set scoring records every year he was there, and despite the fact he signed the largest contract anyone in team sports up until that time had been awarded, he found true success to be elusive. He searched, but the answers he sought wouldn't come. He tried every extreme diet or fad that promised something—anything that might be better. Everything fell short. He painted a message on the roof of his house for the extra-terrestrials to see: "Take me first!" When he was coldcocked outside of a bar after his advances on somebody's sweetheart weren't appreciated, he woke up in the parking lot with a gun stuffed into his mouth. "I'm going to kill you, Pistol Pete, how 'bout that!" was what his assailant said. Pete told us what he was thinking—"Go ahead. At least then I'll have some peace."

Pete had come to understand what Bill Russell had meant when he said, "There is no ultimate victory in sports. There is satisfaction in winning a championship or scoring crown—for a while. But then you've got to do it again." Having experienced the emptiness that follows incredible achievement, maybe being able to relate to Russell's insight as few others can, Maravich became a recluse after he retired from basketball. Until the night he stopped running from God. He knew he had been running toward everything but Jesus, because Pete wanted to control his own life. That night, he admitted he couldn't do that. So he gave his life to the Lord.

Immediately, he set out to find all the people he had ever wronged, lied to, or taken advantage of, so he could apologize to them. If restitution was possible, he did what he could to square things. He was "born-again," and for the last five years of his life, Pistol Pete Maravich did whatever he believed God wanted him to do. Mostly, he looked for opportunities to tell kids his story. He hoped to save them from making the same sinful mistakes. Anyone who heard him during this period of his life gets chills when they remember hearing Pete say, "Today is the time to turn your life over to Jesus. Tomorrow is not guaranteed. I could die of a heart attack when I'm forty for all I know. I think of all the times I could have died. Should have died. And how I had rejected God's provision for salvation and would have deserved hell. Don't wait, please!"

Not long after he visited our Southwestern College team, Pete dropped dead of a heart attack after playing in a half-court pickup game of basketball with Dr. James Dobson and some other weekend warrior-type players. His last words were, "I feel pretty good."

He was forty years old.

CHAPTER 16
LOYALTY AND BUSES

We were rolling! We'd raised $10,000 from the jackets and another $10,000 from the golf tournament. We'd be able to buy uniforms, stay in motels when necessary, hire referees, and even eat while traveling. Transportation was still an issue, but I had an idea I thought would solve that problem. One of the Suns' owners was on the board of directors at Greyhound. The Greyhound corporate offices were in Phoenix, and I felt very optimistic that they might have an extra bus laying around that we could use for a few road trips. So I asked if there was anything they could do to help.

"No."

Not even a discount. The answer was "no." I couldn't believe it. No one is required to say "yes" to a request like ours, of course, but the connection seemed too perfect to be denied. Yet his position remained adamant. Business decision, I suppose.

I couldn't blame him. Long ago I had learned that loyalty can be a one-way street. In the early 1970s, the Celtics were firmly in New England's backseat compared to Boston Bruins hockey. Basketball might sell out when the Lakers or Knicks visited but didn't draw more than 10,000 most nights. For a Thursday night game against a pitiful Cleveland Cavaliers team, they could only hope for about 5,000—if it didn't snow.

Tom "Satch" Sanders was one of the reasons the Celtic Dynasty existed. He and K.C. Jones were the primary "defensive stoppers" in the Russell years. Satch was usually assigned to front court stars like Elgin Baylor, George Yardley, or Bob Pettit, while K.C. drew guards like Jerry West and Oscar Robertson. The Celtic philosophy was to try and cover these unstoppable players with only one man in the hope of minimizing the effectiveness of the non-stars. Satch and K.C. often gave up big numbers, accompanied by low shooting percentages, which added up to victories. Next to the guy who picked up the towels, they had the most thankless jobs in the organization.

Then, like today, home run hitters and big scorers drove Cadillacs, while guys who advance runners and play defense were happy not to be pedestrians. Not that Red Auerbach didn't appreciate the "dirt workers." He publicly praised his defensive role players. He appreciated them, in addition to the fact that the respect and regard he afforded them helped keep the payroll down. When a scorer wanted a raise, Red would go on and on about how important the defenders were and ask how he could possibly pay him out of proportion to the guys who helped the squad so much with defense. Then, when it was time to negotiate with Satch or K.C., Red would turn to his defenders and ask how he could possibly pay them more than he was paying the scorers!

Naturally, the club chose a Thursday night game against Cleveland to honor the soon-to-retire Tom Sanders. The knowledgeable Boston fans' respect for Satch's selfless play over the years produced a sell-out crowd.

"We're going to buy you a new Caddy and present it to you Thursday night at half court," he was told. Tom had never made big NBA money, topping out at roughly $30,000 per year before playoff money was added in. He and his wife, Karen, an airline stewardess, shared a year-old Buick Electra, the GM sister to the very full-sized Cadillacs of the early 1970s.

"Many thanks," he said, "but we really don't need another tank. Do you think we could get a Cougar instead please?" A new Fleetwood was about $10,000, while a Cougar was closer to $6,000. Satch thought he was allowing the club to save a few bucks.

"No, Tom, you don't understand. We don't want to present you with something that looks cheap. We don't want you driving away in anything less than a Cadillac. You deserve it! Oh, by the way, we need you to turn in the Electra because we're only budgeted to spend five grand."

Let's do the math. The game drew 10,000 extra fans for "Satch Sanders Night." At just five bucks per ticket, that's $50,000. After spending $5,000 for the car, they still made a major profit on the evening. Probably enough to pay Satch's entire year's salary. And Karen was without a car.

And we still needed a bus. Then one day, my phone rang. It was Perlin Bull, who had his own small bus business, scratching out a living chartering his bus to groups heading for the Grand Canyon or Las Vegas. "Coach, I hear you could use a bus for a couple of California trips. It's not Greyhound, but I do have a bus and would love to help." He not only provided a bus, but was our driver too.

I can't say I would call it a miracle, but it sure was a blessing. Knowing people like Perlin Bull roam the earth makes the bumps in the road of life a lot easier to take.

There must be something about buses that brings out the best in some people. After all, Walt Rock was driving a bus for Phoenix Country Day School when we met. Then, a year later, after I had become the coach at Grand Canyon College (big move up for me—the job paid $30,000 and the school was a member of the NAIA), Walt had moved on to run a business called "Bob's Auto Shop," and I needed transportation help.

Like most small colleges, the Antelopes program had major budget concerns. The school had a rickety eighteen-passenger bus for us to use that could only be described as a beat-up and phased-out airport shuttle bus. There was a three-game visit to Colorado scheduled and the distance between the schools we were playing was considerable. We had the money in our budget to fly to Colorado, but not enough to get from one city to the next unless we decided to camp out or sleep on the bus. Or maybe we could just not eat.

When Walt found out about our plight, he volunteered to help. He agreed to drop us off at the Phoenix airport and then head north. We knew our hotel in Denver could shuttle us from the airport to our accommodations, so we could get a good night's rest. By the time we awoke in the morning, Walt would be rolling up in our bus after driving all night by himself. Then we would have our bus available for the next four days as we buzzed around the state to our various games. After our final game, Walt dropped us at our hotel, where we slept as he headed south in the clunker for another seventeen-hour drive. When we landed in Phoenix, guess who had the bus at the curb and busied himself helping with our luggage? Walt Rock!

For some reason, a lot of memorable things happen on buses. After I was relieved of my duties as coach of the Suns, I took advantage of my time off to accept the position of unpaid volunteer assistant coach at Chaparral High School in Scottsdale. It was no coincidence that our son, Michael, played there. I went from head coach of an NBA team to offering suggestions, if asked, to Terry Kearney, the Firebird's excellent head coach. I loved every second of my time with him. I believe the feeling was mutual, as he has referred to me as one of the best assistants he ever had!

One of my long-time, firm convictions was that a man should never coach his son. I broke my own rule five years later when I agreed to coach the Pepperdine team that already had Michael as a member, but the way things were arranged at Chaparral was perfect. By being Terry's assistant, I never had to make the tough decisions regarding playing time. I was there as a resource for the coach and to encourage the players. Plus, I got to sit in the front row for every game my son played in his last two years of high school. An incredible blessing.

Coach Kearney was old-school. He had principles, on the floor and off it. He expected his team to abide by them. I learned a lot from him about team defensive philosophy, and I enjoyed how perfectly he allowed the personalities on his team to mesh and flourish. His little squad from Scottsdale played a fearless, aggressive, full-court-pressing, unselfish, relentless brand of basketball. There was seldom a season that they weren't knocking on the door of an Arizona State Championship.

Whenever they played an away game, they rode together on a school bus. When the trip concluded, Terry would remind everyone that they represented not just themselves, but their school and team as well. "Clean up the bus" would always be his final statement as the doors swung open in the Chaparral parking lot.

During Michael's junior year, the Firebirds were knocked off in the state tournament by Moon Valley High School (led by future NBA player Richard Jefferson). The loss hurt badly, but with four starters returning (and Jefferson moving on to the University of Arizona), it was easy to believe that next year would be the year the Firebirds would go all the way. But it didn't work out that way. Even though Chaparral looked like the best team in the state, Moon Valley found a way to knock us out for the second year in a row. It was a hard loss to take. No one spoke on the ride home. Coach Kearney knew his best chance to win the state title that he had been chasing for so many years, had slipped through his grasp—again!

He believed his team was the best in the state. He also knew there would be no mulligans. Sadness was unavoidable, but so was the pride he felt. What were the right words for a team that had fought so long and hard together? This was a team he both admired and loved. And he was feeling the depths of defeat and the height of success. He chose his words carefully. And perfectly.

"Clean up the bus."

Most coaches crave punctuality concerning the team bus. Coach Avery Johnson would have an assistant inform him when all the players were aboard before he would appear and get on. That way, he felt it would never look like he was waiting for a player, and thereby vicariously cede a bit of authority and control. Suns Coach John MacLeod didn't worry about it if a player arrived after he boarded, but if the player wasn't on at least five minutes before the announced departure time, John would look at his watch and say, "Let's go, Driver."

I scored my career-high forty-nine points in a road victory over the Detroit Pistons. I messed up my alarm, and the hotel did the same with my backup wake-up call the next morning. I made it a practice to always be on the bus at least ten minutes early, so when I wasn't there by 8:50, Proski figured that something must be amiss. Nowadays, teams have people in charge of waking up the players. If a player is late, someone is in trouble for failing to wake him up. In those days, though, the players were responsible (as they should be) for themselves. John didn't think the club should be in the wake-up call business, but Proski couldn't bring himself to let me miss the bus, so he made up an excuse to return to the lobby and call my room from a house phone. "Hey, Westy, you okay?"

"Huh? What time is it?"

"Ten 'til."

"Don't let him leave. I can make it!"

I always "packed and sacked." I leapt out of bed, threw on my clothes, grabbed my bags and sprinted out the door without even brushing my teeth. I arrived at the spot where the bus had been—two minutes before the 8:55 time when the 9:00 bus was supposed to leave. I arrived just in time to see the taillights disappear from the hotel parking lot. Even though my cab beat the bus to the airport by at least ten minutes, I had to pay a $100 fine on top of the cab fare. John loved leaving people almost as much as he loved the game of basketball itself.

My own approach as a coach was less severe than MacLeod's, but I still wanted our bus to leave on time. I have left plenty of players, but never by leaving early. During our first Southwestern bus trip, we rewarded the cheerleaders (and ourselves) for their jacket-selling prowess by including them in our traveling party. They had helped us raise enough cash to afford food and lodging, and it was the least we could do to include them on our adventure.

Still, I knew that it was my job to put enough fear in everyone's hearts that punctuality could be achieved. I made it clear that people would be left in the desert, stranded and alone, if they were even one second late for the bus. Apparently, they believed me, because everyone was on the bus several minutes early after our first night on the road. Except Bonnie Buckingham and her roomie, Heidi Fivecoat. Heidi climbed on with a few seconds to spare, with Bonnie right behind. Their hair was still wet. They were breathing hard from hurrying and nerves, but they had made it! So they thought. Knowing that this was Bonnie's first night in a hotel, ever, I decided to have a little fun. I put on my meanest face and blocked the aisle with my leg, stared at my watch for an exaggerated length of time and then looked dead into her eyes.

She broke before I spoke. She was nearly crying, "I'm not late. Am I?"

With the straightest face I could muster, I asked, "Bonnie, did you make your bed?"

As she turned and ran back toward the hotel, she could be heard screaming, "Oh, no! Please don't leave me!"

It was a very different mentality that Charles Barkley demonstrated concerning buses. My "Bonnie strategy" of instilling fear wouldn't work with him. Fines had no effect on Charles, and leaving him would only work if I was trying to make it easier for his next coach to get him to the bus on time. Besides, he was never more than five minutes late. In fact, he was always exactly five minutes late. He had his reasons, and once I figured those out, I was able to institute a rule. The rule wouldn't have flown for John MacLeod, but it was a new day, so "If you try to get on the bus after Charles does, it won't be here" became the law of the land. That rule was a derivative of the Kurt Rambis dress code I had already installed. In his playing days, before he moved on to coaching and broadcasting and the well-tailored free suits that went with those professions, Kurt was the epitome of a comfort dresser. He was, let's say, a bit cheap. He tended to go with jeans and an untucked sport shirt. The code stated that anyone judged to be more sloppily attired than Rambis would be fined. After all, any successful society needs limits.

Fans and autograph-seekers always seemed to know when our bus was scheduled to leave, and Charles was their most-valued target. Signing autographs and posing for photos might seem flattering, and it is, but it gets old real fast, too. Especially once a player figures out that quite a few of the autograph hounds are collecting signatures so they can turn around and sell them on eBay. Many times there would be a few hundred people standing between Charles as he exited the hotel and the door of the team bus. If he tried to be on time, he'd have to sign and pose for about twenty minutes or so before he could climb aboard. Not to mention he was trying to get ready for a game, and as much as he truly enjoyed interacting with fans, it was not the right time for it. So Chuck decided to be habitually late for our bus. That way, he could sling his bag over his shoulder and put his head down as he moved through the crowd without breaking stride. "Sorry, can't stop. I'm late," he would explain. Genius.

Only once did I witness a break in the execution of his routine. He was his usual five minutes late, and as he was climbing up the stairs and the driver was closing the door behind him, someone held up a baby and shouted, "Please, Charles? Just one? For the baby!"

Charles Barkley is one of the most softhearted people I've ever known. But a large part of him also loves to make people think he's a very bad dude. It's one of the contradictions in his nature that makes him so compelling. Acting put out, he stopped, turned back, and growled, "Gimme the kid!"

The baby was passed to Chuck. He goo-gooed with the child, posed for a picture, and signed the shirt the baby was wearing. People ate it up. Many drew closer, hoping to score too. Charles could feel the love of the crowd, I'm sure, as he snarled, "The rest of you can die."

I said, "Let's go, Driver."

CHAPTER 17

RULES

The first team meeting with any group is significant. I usually make sure to outline my expectations for behavior, and also try to give my players an idea of my vision of what a basketball team is supposed to look like. Even though this was to be my first speech to a team as a coach, I had years of experience from which I could draw to know what to say to these young men of Southwestern College.

Certainly, it was important to make a point about being on time. Everything starts with showing up, and showing up on time was "Rule No. 1."

Rule No. 2 involved music. I'd been on enough teams to know that there is a vast difference of opinion regarding the definition of "good" music. Country and hip-hop seldom share the same aficionados. Mix in the Christian elevator music tendencies of our school, and it was obvious that a meeting of the minds regarding music was not going to be achieved. So I made a simple rule. Headphones must be used when listening to music, unless it was either Bob Dylan or John Stewart being played. My favorites, and therefore the best music in the world. The Isaacs hadn't been formed yet, or they would have been approved too. Johnny Cash almost made the cut, but I didn't want to inflict my musical tastes on others.

Maybe I should digress for a bit and explain my list. No need to justify Dylan's presence on it, of course, but unfortunately there are many people whose life is diminished by their ignorance of John Stewart. I first became aware of him due to his membership in the Kingston Trio. They were the most popular group in the country during the time between Elvis and the Beatles. He sang the lead on songs like "The Reverend Mr. Black" and "Greenback Dollar." When the group broke up, John began his career as a singer/songwriter that would produce over thirty albums of thoughtful, humorous, insightful American music.

It would be impossible for me to go past this point without sharing a Bill Russell story. While I was coaching in Seattle, Bill and I would play golf together. One day, logistics called for him to pick me up in his car for our trip to the course. I asked him what cassette he had been listening to.

"The Kingston Trio at the *Hungry i*."

Of course! What else? Which makes this a perfect place to reapply Red Auerbach's wisdom. He was referring to the Boston Garden, but the quote works for music too. "If it's good enough for Russell, it's good enough for you!"

John Stewart's first solo album was rated as one of the Top 10 albums of 1969, by no less than the greatest rock critic of all time, Robert Hilburn, and *Rolling Stone* has it in the all-time Top 200. But critical acclaim didn't translate into sales, and even though he sold enough to keep producing records, the popularity that the excellence of his music deserved eluded him his entire life. Doesn't mean he wasn't great.

When John came to a small club in Boston in 1973, as a member of the Celtics, I was able to arrange a meeting with him. This was our conversation.

"Hi, John."

"Hi, Paul."

"Do you like basketball?"

"Not really. Do you play guitar?"

"No."

Then it was quiet for a long time. I'm sure he forgot our meeting moments after it happened, but I never did. It was more than twenty years before we would meet again, this time in Phoenix. He was there for a concert at Anderson's Fifth Estate. The owner knew I was still a big fan, so he invited me to the show. This time John and I enjoyed a more satisfying conversation. I invited him and his wife, Buffy Ford Stewart, to attend a Suns game the next night.

It would be the first NBA game for both. They had huge smiles as they sat with Cindy in the first row along the baseline by our bench. From their angle, they had a perfect view to observe a statuesque woman, provocatively dressed, descend the stairs from the mezzanine level toward the Suns' bench. Her entrance couldn't be ignored by anyone in the vicinity. She was stopped by a security guard, who was stationed behind the bench. She handed him a note. Cindy, John, and Buffy then observed the guard pass the note to

Charles, who turned and caught the woman's eye. Chuck shook his head "no." The guard directed the woman accordingly. She turned and slowly ascended the stairs, never to be seen again. Just a day in the life of Charles Barkley.

The game was even more exciting than watching Charles be Charles. At one pivotal juncture, the crowd began the familiar chant of "DE-FENSE! DE-FENSE!" to inspire the home team. Cindy had been to hundreds of games in her life and seldom participated in this kind of cheering. She certainly didn't expect our guests to involve themselves by doing so, either. But as the crowd chanted, John and Buffy rose and yelled right along with the fans.

Buffy turned to Cindy and expressed her joy at the crowd's congeniality. "This is just wonderful. What love there is in this place!"

John and Buffy kept right on with the crowd's chant. Cindy leaned toward them to make sure she was hearing them correctly. Yes, she was. They were in fact the only ones in the entire arena chanting, "BE-FRIENDS! BE-FRIENDS!" No wonder they felt so much love.

As the years passed, John and I spent many memorable times together. We watched O.J. Simpson's white Bronco get chased down the 405 from the sofa in our Phoenix den. We took a road trip along Route 66 to the Cadillac Ranch as part of his research about the "Mother Road" for artistic and musical projects he had going. When John ran into a little issue with the IRS, Cindy and I were able to help them through a rough patch by purchasing the song that he wrote, "Daydream Believer," until circumstances changed, and he could buy it back. We got a big kick out of it every time the oldies station on the car radio played the Monkees' version and Cindy and I could exclaim in unison, "Hey, Sweetie, they're playing our song!"

John attended many Suns games while I was the coach, which included waiting in the coach's office after games for me to conclude my postgame responsibilities. After showering, Charles Barkley would usually stop by to say "Hi" or pose for a photo with whoever happened to be waiting around. Once, upon being introduced, shaking hands with John and graciously saying, "Nice to meet you, John," John broke into a huge grin.

"That's a new record!" he announced.

"Huh?" I said.

"I met Sammy Davis Jr. six times. He never remembered me. It was always, 'Nice to meet you, John.' Charles just broke Sammy's record!"

As great as John Stewart's music is, I suppose that his professional problem was summed up by his experiences with Sammy Davis Jr. and Charles Barkley. He was too unassuming. Class seldom sells. After all, Dennis Rodman was known as a good basketball player before he started wearing dresses. His play alone might have gotten him in the Hall of Fame. And it might not have. But he became a shoo-in after he learned how to capitalize on crazy.

Rule No. 2 is a simple, straightforward rule that has followed me to every succeeding coaching position. Only DeMarcus Cousins found a way to circumvent it. His headphones were the most powerful in existence, and as difficult as it is to imagine, he was neither a Bob Dylan nor John Stewart fan. But he still wanted everyone in the room to hear his music, so he would crank the volume past a healthy level of tolerance and lay the headphones on the seat next to him. They blasted clear across the locker room and could even fill the players' section of the plane. When asked to wear his headphones instead of broadcasting with them, it proved to him how unfairly he was being treated. Again. After all, he *was* using headphones to listen to his music. Why did everyone always pick on him?

The final rule I gave my first team was, "Don't be stupid." If one thinks about it, that's about the only rule we should ever need. It covers skipping class. Covers getting technical fouls or arguing with officials. Drugs are stupid. So is missing practice without prior notification and a great reason. Allowing loved ones to disrupt the team's positive chemistry by only cheering for their relative, or making a scene in the stands about playing time? Stupid. Therefore, against team rules.

The year after I left Southwestern, I did have a player break every rule at the same time. He was a very nice young man, yet he managed to accomplish the rare trifecta. As our bus pulled into the hotel, I announced what time we would be leaving for the game. When five o'clock came, he was not aboard. We left him. When he arrived, ten minutes before tip-off, he made the mistake of beginning his explanation with the excuse, "It's not my fault."

"Oh? Why not? I announced the departure time to the whole team when the bus arrived at the hotel."

"But I couldn't hear you with my headphones on."

There it was! A headphone violation, being late, and making a stupid excuse to top it off! Awesome.

At the next practice, he and his roommate got to run some sprints together. Not waking your sleeping roommate is worse than stupid, it's being a terrible teammate. There is no rule about the necessity of being a great teammate. It is above the rules. It is an axiom.

CHAPTER 18
PRAYER IN SPORTS

It was a given that we would be beginning our first meeting with a prayer. How can it be otherwise, when a group of Christians are about to start a journey together? But what does proper prayer look like?

The Bible tells us not to throw up ostentatious public prayers. We're told to go into a closet and lock the door rather than to call attention to our own "holiness." Still, believers are instructed to pray together, so I wanted us to walk the line.

When I was asked to speak at the weekly chapel service for the college, I had used Mark Twain's "The War Prayer" as my text. In it, Twain told of an old man who interrupted a church prayer meeting that was basically a kind of pep rally for the boys who were about to go off to war. The old man listened to the prayers that entreated God to bestow glory and honor upon their cause. Then he proceeded to translate, explaining that for their prayers to be answered, people's hopes and dreams would be destroyed, widows, and orphans would be created and mixed with maimed survivors of the vanquished enemy. Crops, homes, and cities would be destroyed. Victory for "our boys" would result in the horrific suffering of countless people, but the old man explained that God had authorized him to assure the group that their prayer would be answered if that is what they still desired after understanding what their prayer really meant.

Then the congregation dismissed the old man (angel?) from their midst. No need to waste any more time listening to some lunatic, they concluded.

When I was five or six years old, I remember hearing something in Sunday School about how faith can move mountains. We learned with God, all things are possible. That Jesus loves the little children, and theirs is the kind of innocent faith that God is looking for in people. There was something special about the pure faith of a child. Stuff like that. I put it all together, and right there in Sunday School, I devised a plan.

"Dear God, You know that cowboy-and-Indian toy set I asked my parents to buy for me? Well, I have faith in You, so I believe You will put it under the chair in the living room for me to find when I get home from church today. Thank You so much. In Jesus' name, Amen!"

The first thing I did when we got home was sprint into the living room and dive under the chair. I *knew* that my new toys would be there. I had faith—special faith, even—because I was a purehearted child. This was going to be awesome!

Of course, there were no toys there. But I still had faith. I thought maybe God had heard me say to put them under the living room sofa, not chair, so I checked there just in case He hadn't heard me correctly. Maybe this was a mini-test to see if I really had faith. Still, no toys. Just the realization that Bob Dylan would get plenty of agreement from me when he would declare that God is not "an errand boy to satisfy your wandering desire."

As I grew up, I got a little more sophisticated with my prayers. By the time I was ten, I was the best marbles player at Lincoln Elementary School. We would arrive at school a half an hour before class to play. Some liked to "set 'em up" and others liked to shoot. I was a shooter. I brought two marbles every day, just in case I missed with my first shot. Missing twice was inconceivable. How difficult the target determined how many marbles one would receive for hitting it. Typically, a "hit" would mean receiving three to five marbles back. We played for keeps, and I usually entered class with both pockets of my jeans full of marbles.

After a while, this became a problem. The other kids were running out of marbles, thereby, threatening my action. I decided to cut God in. I started selling marbles back to them. I decided that I'd keep half and put the rest in the offering basket at Sunday School. God was my partner, and the games would go on!

I was splitting twenty to thirty dollars a week. Once I sold some marbles to a kid on credit. He avoided me for about a week, so when I saw him, I knocked him down, sat on his chest, and took his lunch money. For Jesus, of course. Except I had forgotten what the boy looked like who owed the money, so I ripped off some poor innocent (and hungry) child.

When I realized my mistake, I did apologize and pay him back. More importantly, I decided right there that I would not become a TV evangelist.

Being a ten-year-old is one thing, but years later, another concept that I had come to be wary of was the pre-game chapel service. When Larry Bird's Celtics and the Sixers of Dr. J. were at the height of their rivalry, the teams hated each other so much that they held separate chapel services. Same chaplain, different meetings. One innocent bystander happened to be outside the door of the Boston group when he heard the leader closing in prayer. He asked God for a Celtic victory. Then he went down the hall to conduct the Sixers' meeting. He also prayed for them to win! I know with God, all things are possible, but come on! I've always been suspicious of team chapel services since that day.

Before our first team prayer, I also recounted the story of the time I was asked to be a part of a "Christian" sports seminar. The featured speaker was a man who claimed that he would teach people how to emulate Jesus as they competed in athletics. His premise was that only by competing as Jesus would compete, could an athlete reach his or her full potential. The speaker's idea was that he and I would play a set of tennis for the attendees to observe. At appropriate times, he would address the audience with relevant insights, such as what Jesus would want us to be thinking, in contrast to how a "secular" competitor might look at things.

When I double-faulted on a serve, someone asked for his thoughts. "Jesus would not be pleased to see his opponent double-fault. He would never take pleasure in another's failure, right, Paul?"

I guess he thought that since I was a Christian, I would rubber-stamp his teaching. "Welllll … I'm not so sure about that," I answered as he gasped. "If Jesus played tennis, I'm pretty sure He would understand that people often double-fault because they respect their opponent's service return so much that they try too hard to deliver an especially excellent serve. Which is a lower percentage play, which leads to more doubles. Part of the game. Hitting a winner is not the only acceptable way to win a point. Jesus would know that."

My opponent continued with the seminar, desperately wishing he had picked someone with a less heathen-like outlook on poor serving, I suspect. But I'll give him credit, he kept plugging away with his theory on Christian tennis. I hit a cross-court winner to his forehand side that hit the side fence after spinning off the line. Even though it was well out of his reach, he kept after it and crashed into the fence in a futile attempt to make an impossible get. Again, the match paused for a question. "Why crash into the fence for a ball you couldn't get?"

"Because Jesus would never quit on a play. Don't you agree, Paul?"

"Welll … maybe Jesus would be indestructible and never get tired. He is God, you know, but if we assume that when He plays tennis, He limits His supernatural powers, I'm pretty sure that He would be smart enough not to waste His energy on a ball He knew He couldn't reach."

I never got invited back to any more of his seminars. But I did make sure our Southwestern team would stop and think about what their prayers meant and would be careful about over-spiritualizing a game. We prayed for God's will, and we prayed that we would trust and obey Him in every part of our lives.

CHAPTER 19
PLAYING TO WIN

With any team I would ever coach, I tried to instill a mentality of how to win. Some teams embraced the idea, some didn't. But the boys on the Southwestern team made themselves wide-open to instruction. Whether at practice, a meeting, while eating or traveling, I tried to use every opportunity to teach.

Having grown up in a competitive home, picking up some principles concerning how to win had been unavoidable. The first tenet of the "Westphal Athletic Code" is that the winner could never quit. He had to allow the vanquished a chance for revenge. And the second pillar of the Code is that a loser could never quit either. In fact, as he issues the rematch challenge, he probably ought to throw in a little trash talk for good measure.

That's all I did during the 1993 NBA Playoffs when we fell behind the Lakers 0–2 in a best-of-five series. Both losses came at home, and we appeared deader than religious freedom in Iran. When I said, "We'll win Tuesday night, and then we play again Thursday. We'll win that one and then come back here and win. And everyone will say what a great series it was," I was only reliving countless backyard reactions on a much larger stage. Competition can only end if the series is over, or one's mother enforces bedtime. Plus, I really believed we were the better team.

One of the most ridiculous cliches regarding competition is, "We want to beat them at their best." To me, that's taking sportsmanship one step too far. John MacLeod tried to inspire us with that line once when Kareem Abdul-Jabbar was suffering from a migraine and appeared doubtful for our game. When he said that, Alvan Adams rolled his eyes, and I could read his thoughts. "That's easy for you to say, John. You don't have to guard him for forty-eight minutes."

Beating someone "at their best" sounds good, but I just want to win when the game is scheduled and move on to the next.

Dan DeReuiter was of the Eli Wallach character's (in *The Good, The Bad, and the Ugly*)[9] persuasion when it came to shooting. "When you gotta shoot, shoot! Don't talk," he told a dead man, who had hesitated a moment before. No matter the score or time on the clock, Dan's answer to the situation was to shoot. I had to explain to him that the idea was to win the game, not to score points.

With our point guard Danny Coyle, I tried to teach him what John Stockton would articulate a few years later. I was the coach of the Western Conference All-Stars in 1995. One of our centers was Dikembe Mutombo, a defensive specialist who thought he could score better than others believed he could. After every time-out, I could hear him muttering that he was open. I approached Stockton and told him what I had heard. "I know," he said. "Can't you draw up any plays where he's *not* open?"

I taught them that there is no shortcut to greatness. I'd seen Alvan Adams make that mistake once. We would play in Buffalo once a year. We loved it when the schedule brought us into town the night before the game. That would always mean one thing—Anchor Bar, here we come. The home of hot Buffalo Wings. They weren't available everywhere in those days, and the first time Alvan sampled them, he downed forty-seven! And the next night, he lit up Bob McAdoo for forty-seven points.

I can't overemphasize how anxious he was to get to Buffalo the next season. Sure enough, the NBA schedule masters were kind to us. We hit town with plenty of time for gluttony, and Alvan didn't disappoint. He downed fifty wings that night. It looked like McAdoo would be in trouble. Unfortunately for Alvan, forty-seven must have been his limit. He became too sick to play the game.

A less-extreme lesson concerning humility and competitive greatness came from something I witnessed tennis great Rod Laver do. He was well past his prime, but since he is arguably the best tennis player ever, he wasn't too shabby when he was in his early forties. Still, appearing in World Team Tennis matches was not what he was born to do.

His team came to Phoenix to play the Phoenix Racquets. Laver was asked to play a set against Butch Walts, a hard-serving young prospect. When Butch served an ace to take a five-love lead in the set, the home crowd

---

9 *The Good, The Bad, and the Ugly.* Directed by Sergio Leone Sergio Leone. 1967. United Artists, Film.

cheered. That was when he made his fatal mistake. True to Team Tennis etiquette, but against the traditional laws of respectful tennis, Butch raised his arms as he bounced up and down and exhorted the crowd to go crazy. After all, he had all but put away the great Rod Laver and it was time to celebrate.

I saw Laver's face change as they switched sides. He allowed himself a sideways dart of his eyes toward his exuberant opponent. Then he looked down at his racquet and focused on rearranging his strings. His jaw tightened. Then he proceeded to carve Butch to pieces. He won seven straight games to take the set. Then he gestured with his racquet his thanks to the referee and politely, but not overly so, shook Walts' hand. He did not smile. He acted as if it were just another day at the office.

After the match, a writer asked him to explain the turnaround. He never mentioned his opponent's hotdogging. What he did do is pass along the advice his old Australian coach, Harry Hopman, had ingrained into his generation of great Aussie players. "When things get tough, go for the lines."

On one of our road trips before we got to travel in a bus, Tim Fultz pulled a "Butch Walts" on me. We were playing chess as we drove across the desert (yes, I was driving … not exactly safe … but funny) and when he beat me, he couldn't help but cry out, "Yesss! I beat Coach. Hey Walt, I beat him! Checkmate! Yesss!"

Well, as you might imagine, as the self-declared "Rod Laver of the chessboard" in that van, I couldn't abide his excessive celebration. "Hey, Walt." I pulled to the side of I-80, "You're old enough to drive a rental. Come on up here and take the wheel so I can ruin the rest of Tim's trip." I'm not proud of it, but I enforced the "Westphal Athletic Code" on him all the way from Gila Bend to Los Angeles. To his credit, he never quit, even though he never beat me again.

Eugene Denning liked the "go for the lines" story. In fact, he didn't really need to hear it, because he always went for the lines, by nature. At the end of every practice, we always had shooting drills combined with conditioning. One of my favorite things to say to my teams was, "If you can't shoot, you gotta run."

After practice one Friday, Gene proposed a bet. "Coach, I have a date tonight. How about if I make this shot from the top of the circle, I get your little Mercedes for the weekend?"

"What do I get if you miss?"

"I'll run sprints."

Even though there weren't any specific rules at our level against me lending a player my car—that I know of—I'm pretty sure there would have been if anyone had thought to write a rule book. I knew for sure that Cindy would have a rule against it if I came home without a car, so I said, "Make it ten sprints and you got a deal."

That figured to be the end of the bet, but the other players started calling him a chicken, so what else could he do? He said, "Deal!"

Now I was the one on the spot. I couldn't say "no" now, so Gene got his shot at my wheels. He made it and was nice enough to give me a ride home that night.

Finally, I wish I could have told them the following story, but it hadn't happened yet. Many years after we had retired, Bill Walton and I limped across the court at the Staples Center from different directions. He could not bend his fused ankles, which combined with other knee, neck, and back injuries he'd picked up along the way, made his gait painful to watch. I walked like a slow-motion version of "Gunsmoke's" Chester. I was overdue for knee and hip replacement and was moving even worse than Bill.

We met near half court and sunk into our chairs to tape a radio interview. As we were beginning, we each felt a hand touch us on the shoulder from behind. It was a mutual acquaintance, who said, "It's hard to believe you guys could *ever* run up and down this court. You're damn near crippled. Was it worth it?"

In unison, with no hesitation whatsoever, UCLA and USC, liberal and conservative, big and small, agnostic and Christian, agreed for one moment. "Ah … yes," we said.

We all know that everyone can't win all the time. And no matter what Disney or Whitney Houston might say, we can't all have our dreams come true if we just wish hard enough. How to compete, striving for the win, that was the message I wanted ingrained. No regrets. Go for the lines.

CHAPTER 20
LANGUAGE

During one of our first practices at La Mancha, I noticed some of our players were throwing around some colorful language. Not under their breath either. The words wouldn't have made a rapper blush, but that doesn't mean the school's leadership would approve. I blew the whistle and directed the team to a meeting room. Then I shared a couple of stories.

The first was about Bayard Forrest, a teammate of mine on the Suns. He and his wife, Peggy, went on to be missionaries, a calling he cut his NBA career short to pursue. Peggy eventually became a faculty member at both Southwestern and its later incarnation, Arizona Christian University. Ever since I've known Bay, he was always a committed and serious Christian man. One day, he was having a tough practice. Sometimes his frustration would boil over, and he could be heard to say with some measure of disgust toward himself, "Shoot!" After a few such mutterings, Coach John MacLeod called the team together.

"What did you say, Bayard?"

"I said 'shoot,' Coach."

"Why?"

"Because I keep messing up, and I'm frustrated."

"You are struggling, Bayard. But are you sure that you didn't say 'sh—?' Because you're playing like sh—."

"I said shoot."

"It's okay to say sh—, Bayard. My wife says sh—. If it applies, you *should* say 'sh—.'"

"It means the same thing to me, Coach, but I did say shoot."

After practice ended, I'll never forget hearing Alvan Adams call out to Bayard as "Big Bay" was among the first players to head for the locker room. From the other end of the gym Alvan hollered, "Hey, Bay. Don't go yet. Let's stick around and sh— some free throws!"

John Wooden used to say, "Goodness, gracious sakes alive! What was that, Walton?" With the veins in his neck showing. No drill sergeant's profanity-laced berating could top Coach Wooden's intensity, yet he chose family friendly words. But it meant the same to him. Tommy Heinsohn dropped, by my actual count, seventy-three "F-bombs" during his half-time talk to the Celtics on Christmas Day, 1974. After the first fifty or so, the shock value disappeared.

"I like your intensity. Nobody wants to take it away. But please stop yelling 'sh—' while you represent Southwestern Conservative Baptist Bible College, okay?"

They did.

"Taking God's name in vain is a bit different than figuring out where to draw our lines on colorful language, though," I told them. "But even there, people have to figure out what the biblical admonition concerning this means. I keep God out of any questionable phrases, but I actually believe that those who pervert God's truth for their own gain are far more guilty of 'taking God's name in vain' than someone who asks God to obliterate his putter for making him four-putt from fifteen feet again."

Language is a strange thing. Words are just words. But words reveal what is in the heart. That's what the Bible says. The last thing I want is for God to check my heart and have it be full of ... uh, not good stuff!

CHAPTER 21
PRESS CLIPPINGS

Our practices at La Mancha were on display for anyone who happened into the building between two and five on weekdays. Joggers circled the court on the indoor track. At one end, people used the weight machines that looked out over the basketball floor. At the other end was a restaurant that also had a view of the proceedings. Cindy would sometimes drop by, where she often heard onlookers say things like, "Isn't that Paul Westphal out there with those high school kids? Or are they junior-highers?"

We pretty much started with "This is a basketball" and went from there. Some of the guys never got much further than that. Others seemed to absorb everything, and by the time our first game arrived, we were comfortable with our UCLA high post offense, 1-2-1-1 and 2-2-1 full-court presses, 1-3-1 and 3-2 zones and a switching man to man defense.

One of our first games was against American Indian Bible College. We loved playing them because they always brought about 200 fans along. Admission was free, but we cleaned up selling candy at the snack bar when the AIBC came to town.

We started off a little nervous, and AIBC jumped off to a 5–0 lead. Their fans were going nuts, stomping on the wooden bleachers of Desert Cove Middle School like they'd never been stomped before. Pandemonium! A person would have sworn that there were ten times as many cheering, it was so loud.

It was then that I called what I believe to be the most-effective time-out in basketball history. Seriously.

"Okay," I said, "Let's start pressing full court. 1-2-1-1 after free throws, 2-2-1 after field goals."

We ran off forty-seven straight points.

And when they finally scored again, making the score 47–7, they went nuts again. Just as loud as before! Why can't all fans be like those of American Indian Bible College?

One never knew what to expect when we got to a gym for a game. There was no budget for advance scouting, and even a VHS tape of an opponent was almost impossible to come by. Sometimes we might be evenly matched, sometimes we were the far superior squad (like we were with AIBC), and other times, we were way overmatched. Christ College of Irvine twice beat us as badly as we had beaten AIBC. Same with West Coast Christian. Arizona Auto, where future Utah Jazz star, seven-foot, four-inch Mark Eaton had once matriculated, showed up to play wearing "uniforms" consisting of yellow T-shirts with numbers drawn on with magic marker and any shorts they could find. They were so frustrated by losing to our ragtag group that one of their players on the bench stood and mooned our fans in disgust.

The *Los Angeles Times* ran an article about me before our game in Fullerton against Pacific Coast Christian College. Even though virtually no one except family and a few very close friends of the home team ordinarily would have attended that game, there was a surprise waiting in the stands when we got to the gym. Seated right behind our bench was actor/director Dennis Dugan and a friend of his. They comprised our entire rooting section, and when they saw us enter, Dennis and his friend started cheering wildly and doing the wave. As far as I know, it was the only two-man wave in history.

A few years earlier, while I was with the Knicks, Mike Lupica took me to the famous New York media hangout, Elaine's. There we met Dennis, who just happened to be in town for a couple of days. Mike and I shared a love of anything James Garner ever did or would do, and "The Rockford Files" was his hit show at the time. We immediately recognized Dennis from his recurring role as Richie Brockelman (boy detective). They even spun off a show by that name. It didn't last, but it should have.

Mike and I hit it off with Dennis. When I offered him tickets to the next night's game, he accepted. I never saw him again until four years later when I walked into that gym in Fullerton. There he was, standing, sitting, standing, sitting, waving his arms, and screaming.

"What the hay, it's Dennis Dugan!" I said when I recovered from the shock of what I was seeing. "What the hay" was Richie Brockelman's catchphrase. Now that I really think about it, maybe that show wasn't quite as good as I thought.

"We read about your game in the *Times*. Took us two-and-a-half hours to get here from the Palisades, but I figured if I can be there at the Garden, while you're on top, then I can drive to Fullerton and be here when you're on the bottom."

By the way, for whatever it's worth, Dennis is very left-leaning politically. So is Mike Lupica. Just like I was once. It happens. Both are famous, and both have been close, trusted friends. Yet no media person has *ever* grilled me about my relationship with either of them, or any of my other liberal friends. So why was it considered to be such a mortal sin to be friends with Rush Limbaugh? I truly believe my friendship with Rush hurt me in ways that can't be measured in both of my post-Phoenix NBA head coaching jobs.

Openly left-wing sportswriters in Seattle and Sacramento intentionally falsified "facts" to discredit my coaching. I'm sure there were plenty of things about my coaching they could have found lacking, so why did they need to make up stuff? One writer for the *Seattle Times* built an entire column on three verifiably incorrect things that did not happen. He wrote his column as if they had, serving his agenda of making me look incompetent. I had always respected his opinion before this incident, going back to my days as a player, so I asked to meet with him and seek an explanation for his sloppy work.

"Steve, I can understand that you have a right to your opinion concerning my coaching. It's your job. But you built your entire column on three things that did not happen. Then you used those lies to 'prove' what a bad coach I am. That's not fair, and I'm very disappointed. It was either very lazy, or very unethical. Which was it, and now that you know the truth, what are you going to do to correct the record?"

"Paul," he answered, "sometimes when a columnist wants to come out with a certain conclusion, he uses whatever he needs to get there."

We never spoke again. What does one say to someone who admits that truth takes a backseat to his agenda?

I happened to run into Steve again, though. After the SuperSonics let me go, I hit my favorite breakfast place, the Five Spot, on my way out of town. Sitting two booths away, with his back to me, there he was, eating by himself. I called his waitress over and paid for his breakfast. He turned to see who had decided to pick up his check. He had a big smile on his face as he turned, and I wish I could describe what happened to his expression when he realized who had treated him. Whatever that look was, it wasn't a smile anymore. I nodded and headed to my car for the drive south to our home in Los Angeles. He was still sitting there last time I looked.

There have been many lazy or incompetent media people who just try to do their jobs and don't mean any harm, and a few excellent journalists who have taken their craft to the level of art. But there has only been one other writer who I'm sure knowingly lied about me: a columnist for the *Sacramento Bee*. One of her pet ploys was to go around to the families and agents of players who might not have played as much as they would have liked. Then she would use them as "unnamed sources close to the situation" to sow as much discord as possible. Being an ardent feminist and far-left progressive, she welcomed me to town with relentless allusions to my impossible-to-understand (for her) friendship with Rush Limbaugh. Even after I explained Rush and I had hardly been in touch for several years, and that I had many liberal friends as well, she couldn't let it go. She was reprimanded, and almost fired for fabricating quotes that reflected poorly on my coaching. I firmly believe she tried to get me fired, and that my conservative political beliefs made me an acceptable target in her mind.

So maybe I can't prove these ardently progressive scribes targeted me because of Rush. What I do know, however, is that before or since, I have never had people write what they know to be lies about me. Coincidence? I think not.

CHAPTER 22
THEOLOGICAL ISSUES

On another of our road trips to California, we slept on the floor at Howard Slusher's house in Rolling Hills. At least, the players did. I got a bed. Howard lived on two acres overlooking the Pacific with a fantastic view of Santa Catalina Island. He had a tennis court, a pool, and a game room that included video games, a pool table, a popcorn machine, a wet bar, an ice cream bar, and a vintage slot machine. Nobody drank his alcohol, including Howard, but they sure loved posing for pictures with an unopened can of beer while standing by the slot machine. Or leaning on his Rolls-Royce.

Howard's son, John, was almost as crazy as Howard. Once, while Howard was on a business trip, John removed some plate glass windows from the living room, so he could park their Volkswagen Karmann Ghia where the coffee table had been. Then, he replaced the windows. It gave Howard's home just the right ambiance to make a house full of college kids feel right at home. They ran around the house shooting rubber bands from Howard's rubber band gun at each other, frolicking in the pool and just generally enjoying life with Slush.

Part of our stay included a trip to Santa Anita Racetrack where Howard was part-owner of a horse that would be racing that day. Some of them thought there was a good chance we would be in the presence of gambling if we went, and wondered if the college would approve. But I didn't have the president's cell phone number (maybe because nobody had cell phones in those days), and we couldn't very well be ungrateful houseguests, could we? So we went to the track. Howard paid everyone's admission. His horse won. I didn't see any of our players gamble. No one ever asked if we went to the track. And since we continued to play all the games that remained on our schedule, I conclude that nobody ever found out.

I believe many at the school back then would have canceled basketball if they could have. There was an anti-basketball sentiment alive at Southwestern College in the 1980s. One student told one of our players that the team was a bad influence on the other students. An "ungodly" distraction. And the whispers became much louder after our game against Arizona College of the Bible.

Since they were our hated cross-town rivals, we secured the Shadow Mountain High School gym for the game. After all, we might have as many as three hundred for this clash to secure local Bible college bragging rights. The game eventually went into double overtime, and when the roller coaster of a game ended, we had prevailed. We basked in the afterglow of the win on Sunday. On Monday morning, I received an unexpected call from the president. And it wasn't to congratulate me for wrecking ACB's Sunday. "Paul, we need to talk. Can you please come by my office as soon as possible?"

"Sure. I'll be right there."

When I arrived at his office, I could tell that things were looking bleak, but I had no idea why. Thankfully, he was straightforward about the situation. "There is a strong feeling among some influential people that the basketball program is not something that is good for our school. It seems to be promoting too much un-Christian behavior. It might be best that we cancel the rest of the games. Sorry."

"Un-Christian behavior?"

"Jeff Nimtz received a technical foul. I understand that he threw a ball against a wall and directed some profanity toward an official. That kind of thing is unacceptable."

"I spoke to Jeff about it. He did lose his temper, and he felt very bad about it. Until a person has been the recipient of some bad calls in the heat of competition, it's hard to understand how difficult it can be to simply accept them. Technicals are part of the game, as is learning how to overcome bad calls and manage emotions. Jeff is an intense competitor and a great kid. Surely we can get past this, can't we?"

"If that was all," the president said, "I'm sure we would. Jesus displayed anger when he turned the money changers' tables over, even though I'm sure we agree that this isn't quite the same thing."

"Actually, I'm not sure referees aren't even more obnoxious than money changers."

He continued. "People are also concerned about some un-Christian behavior that has been displayed by our cheerleaders and some of our students. They were positioning themselves behind the basket while the other team was shooting free throws. They were waving their arms and yelling to distract the shooter and cause a miss. That does not demonstrate good Christian sportsmanship. We should be encouraging both teams, not contributing to rooting for failure, even if they do play for our opponents."

"The best player I ever played with was John Havlicek of the Boston Celtics. Once he told me that, like everyone else, he enjoyed hearing the cheering of fans. He said the best feeling came when he would make an important shot in front of a noisy, hostile crowd in the other team's building. 'The silence,' he explained, 'that was the best sound of all.' Sir, we wouldn't want to deprive any competitor, whether on our team or not, of the chance to experience the joy of what Havlicek described, would we? In my opinion, *that* would be more un-Christian than showing passion and challenging opponents to rise to the occasion."

"Okay. I can relate to what Mr. Havlicek said. Only I feel like I'm the one shooting the free throw in a hostile environment, and the anti-basketball folks are trying to make me miss by deciding to cancel the season," the president admitted. "You have convinced me. I hope we're right. But I still don't like those technical fouls one bit."

"Thanks. Neither do I."

I left, still having a team to coach. But I never was sure if it was my logic that prevailed, or the fact that he secretly enjoyed us kicking ACB's butt.

CHAPTER 23
AN IRONIC TWIST

If I only could have seen the future. About twenty-five years after leaving Southwestern, Cindy and I met gospel music giants Gloria and Bill Gaither. Bill has been called "The Babe Ruth of Gospel Music," a title that suits him well. And as a sports fan, he would admit that he might have been enjoying the title a bit too much, until Gloria reminded him that the Babe still holds the record for most times striking out. He is a man of many interests, and basketball is one of them. In 2013, Bill invited me to visit him at his home in Alexandria, Indiana. Gloria was on a speaking trip, so Cindy stayed in California, so Bill and I could enjoy some time together hanging out.

The Gaithers are legendary figures, though underappreciated in the secular world. Bob Dylan once lamented that he tried, and came up short (so far), in his attempt to write a "specifically religious" song along the lines of "Just A Closer Walk With Thee." Bill and Gloria have done it many times over! "He Touched Me," "Loving God and Loving Each Other," "There's Something About That Name," and "Because He Lives" only scratch the surface of their incredible resume. Not to mention the fact that Jake Hess (Elvis Presley's favorite singer) was in their group, along with other major gospel talents such as Larnelle Harris and David Phelps. They produced a who's who of Christian artists including Amy Grant, Michael W. Smith, Sandi Patty, The Isaacs, The Martins, The Nelons, and Buddy Greene. Secular music can be so snobbish in its devaluation of non-secular artists, but those with open minds will eventually come to the realization that the Gaithers' contributions to American music belong in the same conversation as other contemporaries such as Johnny Cash, Bob Dylan, Paul Simon, and John Stewart.

The Gaither Vocal Band was asked to sing the "Star-Spangled Banner" prior to Game 5 of the 2013 Eastern Conference Finals between the Pacers and Knicks. Bill invited me to come to the game and then spend a day with him. All I can say is, my advice to anyone who gets that call is "don't even think about not going." From the time the seventy-seven-year-old Bill picked me up at the airport to when he dropped me off for my return flight some thirty hours later, my visit was a non-stop eclectic delight.

Bill bounced from the Pacers to politics, touching on music history, the JFK assassination (he had just finished reading a book alleging that LBJ did it), the Isaacs project he was finishing up, childrearing, how much he loves Gloria despite all her faults (just kidding, Gloria), Peyton Manning, and coping with the hilarious Mark Lowry. We only had two near-accidents resulting from his interesting driving before we arrived at the arena about ninety minutes before game time.

Bill is a Pacers season ticket holder, and he makes the drive from Alexandria to catch as many games as his schedule allows. He is as unassuming and low-key as possible, but nearly everyone in Indiana recognizes him as he passes through the crowd. He greets ushers, elevator operators, parking attendants, and waitresses as we move along, always with a genuine patience and humility that one can't help but notice and admire. Kindness is awesome, and the slightly befuddled, self-deprecating, people-loving, God-fearing persona he projects from the stage is no act. It's him.

We ate a quick meal at a buffet set up for early-arriving season ticket holders. Bill was grateful the Pacers picked up the tab for him and his group, in appreciation for their performing the anthem. I thought it was the least they could do, especially since Bill paid to fly David Phelps, Michael English, and Wes Hampton, three-fifths of the Gaither Vocal Band, from Nashville to Indianapolis so they could sing the Anthem before they flew back to Nashville after the first quarter. Bill and I stayed to watch every minute, though, along with Doug, a local singer who Bill enlisted to fill Mark Lowry's spot in the Vocal Band for the night, rather than asking Mark to fly in from Houston for one song.

After the Pacers dismantled the Knicks, Bill drove us to his home. It was the same house he and Gloria bought close to fifty years ago, when they both taught at the local high school. The piano where they composed "He Touched Me," and many more classics, sits in a corner just like a regular piano. "We raised our children here and just never moved. Don't plan to either. But we have added on some over the years."

Their home was "Indiana down-to-earth" style. Lived in and totally unpretentious. But, like Bill and Gloria, there's a lot more there than one might first notice. "I was raised in a little farmhouse a few blocks from here.

We've been in this house our whole married life. We could obviously live in a better house, but this is our home. We do have a nice condo in Nashville, though." He chuckled.

We talked, ate some rum raisin ice cream, and got to bed about a half an hour past midnight. "Paul, I have a meeting in the morning that I need to attend. You can sleep in, and then we'll go get some breakfast when I return around 7:30, okay?

"Great," I said. *You call that sleeping in?* Seventy-seven years old, but he burns the midnight oil and rises with the roosters. Smiling all the time.

The next day, we did what Bill called "relaxing." After he returned from his dawn meeting, we went to breakfast at "Gloria's Place," which is a small part of the Gaither Headquarters in Alexandria. Bill led me on a tour of their store, a treasure trove of antiques, art, doodads, trinkets, books, music, and country charm. Not all "Gaither gear" necessarily, but if that's what you're after, you can find it there. Behind the store is where their tour buses are kept and maintained. There is also a huge warehouse where the DVDs, CDs, sheet music, and other items are stored before being shipped all over the country (and world).

"How many people work here, Bill?" I wondered.

He never hesitated. "Almost half of 'em."

He never did give me a number. But I sure got introduced to plenty of employees, and they all seemed busy to me. He showed me where the master recordings are archived, offices, sound studios, storage rooms, and display cases full of photos, Grammys, and Dove Awards. There were boxes of Dove trophies piled in a utility closet next to a heater. "We have quite a few of those," Bill admitted. The complex was huge, but not nearly big enough. They will need to build a museum to house the mementos necessary to tell the story of the history that gospel music lovers would find fascinating. "I think it will happen, but who has the time to do it?" Not Bill.

In his office were pictures with Billy Graham, various presidents, friends like Larry Gatlin, kids, grandkids, sports stars like Peyton Manning, lots of Gloria, vintage gospel greats, and all sorts of music legends from many genres. But one prominent photo drew my eye. It was a publicity picture of a menacing, shirtless man, knees bent, and arms spread. It was pro wrestler Dick the Bruiser, right there on the wall with a who's who of American Bible Belt icons.

"What's Dick the Bruiser doing on the same wall as Johnny Cash and Hovie Lister and the Statesmen?" I asked.

"When I was a kid, I loved pro wrestling. It was fake, of course, but what a show it was! And it was still very physical, that's for sure. You'd have to be crazy to get in the ring against a guy like Dick the Bruiser. I saw him wrestle in person once. They had a couple of preliminary bouts, tame stuff, and then *he* got introduced and made his entrance. The place went wild. He sauntered into view, but never bothered to climb into the ring. He grabbed his poor opponent, yanked him through the ropes and out of the ring, and then proceeded to start banging his head on the turnbuckle. Then he just left the guy lying there, was declared the winner, and then headed for the showers. It was great!"

What is it about iconic Christian musicians from the Midwest who were kids in the '40s? Bill Gaither grew up in Indiana and loved Dick the Bruiser, while over in Minnesota, Bobby Zimmerman (aka Bob Dylan) was admiring the work of Gorgeous George.

Bill wasn't through telling Bruiser stories. "I knew someone who had a memorable conversation with him once. They were in a bar he frequented, and the conversation went like this. 'Hi, Mr. Bruiser. Glad to see you're back in town. Where'd you go?'

"'Toronto.' His voice was a whisper-growl. As it should be.

"'Why were you there?'

"'Why do you think?'

"'Oh. Heh, heh. Sorry. Who'd you rassle?'

"'Some bum.'

"'How'd you do?'

"'How do you think I did?'

"In the early 1990s, I heard he was living in Indianapolis, so I got his number and called him. I identified myself when he answered, and he said, 'You're that gospel singer guy who's always on TV. I know who you are. I wish my manager was here. He loves you guys!' That made my day. We had a great conversation, and I asked him if he had any tapes of himself wrestling. 'Sure, out in the garage.' I had some ideas, but nothing connected. He passed away about six months later."

We finished the tour of Gaither Headquarters, drove past the water tower that read, "Alexandria, Home of Bill and Gloria Gaither," and headed for lunch with Bill's friend, Rodney, a former Golden Gloves champion who was the Madison County Prosecutor. Then a tour of Anderson University, their alma mater, and on to a drive-by of Alexandria High School. We next visited the house where he was raised, met his sister, and visited their cabin in the woods. Then we stopped to view the magnificence of the "World's Largest Paintball," a must-see attraction for all who visit the area.

I was ready for a nap, but Bill looked at his watch and announced, "If we leave now, I think we can make it to the brickyard by 4:30." So we did. We had time to check out the Indianapolis 500 Museum, as well as wander out to the track and watch the cars zoom around at more than two hundred miles per hour as they prepared for the upcoming Indy 500. Fantastic. By then it was time for dinner. We shared a great meal, and then it was time for him to drop me off at the airport and drive about a hundred miles back to his home.

All that to say, if the people who wanted to cancel basketball at Southwestern had known I was someday going to be blessed with the friendship of Gloria and Bill Gaither, I doubt they would have been so rash.

CHAPTER 24

HEART

When the Southwestern College regular season ended, we had won seventeen games and lost eight. The conference tournament was to be held in Phoenix, with the team that won heading straight to Bristol, Tennessee, for the National Association of Little Colleges Championship Tournament.

Christ College had romped through our league. The only team that had come within twenty points of them, West Coast Christian, didn't have enough money to send their team to Phoenix. Christ College was so confident of their destiny that they arrived in Arizona with non-refundable airline tickets to Tennessee. Meanwhile, we weren't looking ahead. We focused on winning our first Western Association of Christian Colleges conference tournament game against Life Bible College of Pasadena.

The gym at Phoenix Christian High School seemed emptier than I expected when we arrived. Even though it was over an hour before tip-off, I thought there would be more activity swirling around. This was the conference tournament, after all. An hour before tip-off, the gym was still empty, except for our group. No officials, no locker room attendants, nobody but us. What was going on? I started to worry. Unless we were playing either the Indians or ACB, we weren't exactly a big drawing card. But still, even the other team wasn't there! Finally, I had to cop to the possibility that I was leading my team into battle at the wrong gym.

Somehow, we figured out where we were supposed to be and made it over to the Phoenix School for the Deaf Gymnasium in time to avoid a forfeit. We even won the game, which most likely would be our last win of a wonderful season, since our next opponent was Christ College.

They were led by 6'7" center Derwin Appleberry. He could have easily been a Division I player, and they had other good athletes and shooters to complement his dominating presence. But we showed up anyway, despite having been trounced by them twice already.

Our only chance to win would be to collapse our defense around Appleberry and make someone else beat us. They had shooters, but still, we couldn't afford giving him layups and free throws. We gambled on making their shooters hit shots. Offensively, we spread the floor like Dean Smith of North Carolina used to do when he got a lead. We killed the clock until they got too aggressive in attacking us. Then we burned them with dribble penetration or backdoor plays. The key was that we needed a lead to play out our strategy. When that happened, Christ College had to start chasing us, and they never caught us. We had taken a page from Pete Carril's story—we stole their hat!

If we had played them twenty more times, they probably would have won all twenty. But we didn't have to play them again. In fact, since their season was now over, they wouldn't be needing their plane tickets anymore, so I was able to negotiate a smokin' deal on them. Christ College now knew what pool player "Cornbread Red" must have felt like after losing his Cadillac to the legendary hustler Minnesota Fats. "Mr. Cornbread," Fats consoled as he handed the man enough for a train ticket. "You arrived in town a happy motorist, but now you will be leaving a pedestrian."

Our nemesis, Arizona College of the Bible, awaited us in the finals. We would have to beat them to be able to use those tickets. We were now able to do something very special and rare—make the school spend money on basketball. The only request I had made when I took the job was that the college would fund our trip to Bristol if we earned the right to go. It was such a long shot that the president never worried about the risk he was taking. Now, he could possibly lose what amounted to the first bet of his life. His mixed emotions must have been tearing him up. I believe he wanted us to win, and I'm positive he wanted to crush ACB (even though he was far too poker-faced to ever admit it). But still, the trip was going to cost the school a lot of cash, even with the discounted air travel I'd arranged.

The gym at the Phoenix School for the Deaf wasn't packed, but the three-hundred or so that attended made for a nice, non-empty atmosphere in the small venue. We had split our two games with ACB during the year, with both in doubt right down to the end. This time, we got off to a good start and it looked like we would enjoy a wire-to-wire victory.

Our lead stayed steady for the entire game. It fluctuated just slightly, staying between six and ten points. Late in the second half, the game felt like it was well in hand. I didn't worry too much when Dave Narloch fouled out with less than two minutes to play. After all, Bret Foudray was such a reliable sixth man that I thought of him as one of our starters. All season long, until Gene Denning had to leave school, we had relied on seven players for any game that was in doubt. Now we had six, but it looked like that would be enough.

With about a minute to go and our lead at eight points, Dan DeReuiter committed his fifth foul. When the official came over and said it was time to replace him, I thought quickly. "I'd rather not," I said. I knew what the situation called for, and I knew who we had on our bench. The last minute figured to be a free throw shooting contest. All we needed to do was refrain from fouling, make them take outside shots if possible, keep from turning the ball over, and make our free throws when they fouled in desperation because they can't allow the clock to run out. "We'll just finish with four."

"You can't do that. If you have eligible players on the bench, the rules say you must put one into the game."

I thought I might have a loophole with the word "players." But I didn't bother making that argument. Cotton Fitzsimmons would often say to Lionel Hollins and me when we were his assistants with the Suns, "Train, Westy. I want you to always remember this. In fact, write it on my tombstone when I'm gone. 'You can't have too many shooters!'"

Even though I hadn't heard Cotton say it yet, I knew he was right. As I perused our bench, it was apparent that there was trouble in River City. We had a few Chenaniah guys, Marvin the soccer player from Costa Rica, Bob Nedimyer (who had missed more practices than the singers), Justin Cawood (who had suggested we hold our last practice outdoors, it being such a nice day and all, so he could work on his tan—and a terrible foul shooter to boot), Glen Strutz (small, but slow), and Tim (Chevy Nova) Fultz. None had ever played in "crunch time," and this was definitely crunch time.

I picked Tim. He had been to every practice. He often worked on his free throws while the players he would drive back to campus showered. None of the bench players were high-percentage foul shooters, and something made me pick Tim.

"Tim, get in there! Don't foul, and try to stay away from the ball so they don't foul you, okay?"

"Yes, sir, Coach!"

Only college kids say "Yes, sir" anymore. Sometimes. The only pro to ever say that to me was Elliot Perry. Charles Barkley heard it and almost keeled over laughing. But Elliot was raised like that. And so was Tim.

But it didn't stop him from fouling an ACB player as he went for a rebound on his first play in the game. And even though he did stay away from the ball on offense, nothing could stop ACB from fouling him anyway. This was before the "Shaq rule," where a team is penalized for fouling away from the ball in the last two minutes of a game. It was to their advantage to foul Tim—and foul they did.

When he stepped to the line, everyone could see how nervous he was. But he had practiced his free throws, and I thought he shot them with confidence. He missed the first, though. And the second. In fact, he missed *seven* in a row. Didn't choke, just missed, and even though they didn't score every time Tim missed another free shot, they did score enough to make it a one-point game when they fouled him again with three seconds to go. The pressure was tremendous. Their fans were screaming for him to miss. Ours were checking their theology to see if it was okay to pray for him to make it. And most were praying anyway, just in case.

Tim swished both! The fans went wild as they carried him off the floor and threw him in the shower, chanting "Tim! Tim!" all the way. We squirted soda on each other and laughed at how good we all felt. Who knew a trip to Bristol, Tennessee, could generate such joy?

Tim Fultz hadn't gone to college to be a basketball player. Yet he now was the hero of a college basketball game. Hero of an entire season, even. Strange things happen in life. It was a great memory, and after a while, everyone moved on.

Four seasons later, I was an assistant coach for the Phoenix Suns. Tim had graduated and became a missionary to Zaire. When he would come back to Arizona on furlough, Cindy and I would send him back with Nikes we diverted from our basketball camp (thanks again to Howard Slusher and Phil Knight).

Then one day Tim fell off the roof he was constructing for a church in Zaire. After being rushed to the hospital, he was pronounced brain-dead because of his fall. His wife of less than a year, Norma, arranged for the doctors to harvest as many organs as possible. When news of the tragedy reached the Arizona papers, the headline read, "Missionary Boy Leaves Heart in Africa."

Somewhere in Africa, Tim's heart beats in a person who couldn't live without it. The Bible says that where one's treasure is, their heart will be also. We can "lay up treasures in heaven, where moth and dust does not corrupt." It's not our gold that goes with us when our days here end. While he figuratively put his heart into our team, Tim literally gave his heart to the African people—in the name of Jesus.

In Phoenix, news of his death led to numerous donations in his memory to Southwestern College. It was in the brand-new auditorium, part of which would become the Tim Fultz Memorial Gymnasium, that Tim's father, Pastor Larry Fultz, addressed the packed building during the memorial service. "When we used to go on family hikes, even though Tim was not our oldest, he would always jump out ahead of the rest, exhorting us to follow him as he led the way. That's what he's doing now. Tim is in heaven because he followed Jesus. That's the path Tim is showing us." I have no idea how Larry had the emotional control to stay tear-free as he spoke those words. Everyone was crying except him. That's how sure he was that he'd be seeing his son again.

Arizona Christian University is not the only place Tim Fultz's name is associated with a building. In Zaire, the structure he fell from was completed. Larry Fultz traveled there to speak at that dedication as well.

MAN IN WHITE

Larry once told me about an experience Tim had while overseeing a shipment of supplies as they were being delivered to Zaire. Tim was to oversee a particular shipment from me with shoes, basketballs, and various sports supplies. He placed them in a mission van along with some medicine and other valuables and began driving. The medicine was to be flown to a hospital in Vanga, so Tim had to drive it to an airport he was unfamiliar with. He made a wrong turn, ending up on the runway. But the plane to fly the supplies was right in front of him. As he drove closer, several men came toward the van. Tim was pulled out and beaten black-and-blue as they were stealing all the supplies on board. As this ruckus was taking place, Tim said, "A huge man dressed all in white, like an ice-cream man, came from out of nowhere and started throwing these men out of the van. He was amazing. I've never seen anything like it before." Tim continued, "He spoke exceptionally good English, gave me his name and said he worked in the control tower at the airport." Tim made sure the supplies were safely on the plane to Vanga, then looked to thank the man who was no longer there. So

Tim went to the control tower to find him. No one knew his name and said no one who fits his description works there.

"I think he was an angel," Tim concluded. "I had all this medicine that needed to be delivered, and all these supplies for other deliveries that would have been lost had it not been for this man dressed in white."

That leads to an obvious question—if the angel could rescue the much-needed supplies, why couldn't an angel break Tim's fall a few months later? Larry's conclusion, of course, was that an angel could have, but didn't. It was Tim's time. Just like one day, all of us will have it be our time.

With that knowledge in mind, Larry Fultz spoke to the people in Africa who attended the service at the spot where Tim died. Larry told the people he was glad that the building had been completed. It was a wonderful building. "But ..." he said. "I would not have traded my son's life so this church could be constructed. That is not a bargain I would make. I would not have sent my son to you if I would have known he would die. But God would. And did. He sent His son, knowing He would die, so we might live. That's what Tim believed, and that's why he came all the way to Africa—to share that message."

CHAPTER 25
MESSAGE RECEIVED

I made sure my SuperSonics understood Tim's journey. The commitment, respect, and yes, heart, that exemplified his life. Much like Pistol Pete Maravich, minus the basketball acumen, he lived his life with both eyes on the real future, the only future that matters. Eternity.

Chasing fame and money makes one selfish. Following the lead of Pistol and Tim makes one free. Still, it wasn't difficult to discern that my days as the SuperSonics' coach were nearing an end. I shared the story of Tim Fultz and the Southwestern experience with them in hopes that some might someday have an epiphany. At the very least, I hoped they could grasp that there are things more important than self-seeking individualism.

The story of the drama Vin Baker put himself through, and all around him, has only been partially reported. It has been written that many years after retiring, with most of his money gone, Vin was able to give up alcohol and begin to lead a life devoted to helping others avoid the pitfalls that derailed his career. My friend author Andy Andrews says that experience is not the best teacher. Learning from *other* people's experience is. It hurts less. Cheaper, too. Many things that happened behind closed doors with that group have only been hinted at and will remain obscure here as well. But I will elaborate on incidents that have previously been reported to allow truth to breathe.

A short time before I was fired in Seattle, Gary Payton had exploded at me during a game in Dallas. He was one of the more volatile players ever, and in some ways, it was just "Gary being Gary." But the public nature of this explosion made it something that couldn't be left without consequences.

Because of their agents, the Goodwin brothers, Gary and Vin shared a bond that they seemed to value more than winning. Regretfully, I had, at times, let my coaching decisions be unduly influenced by the politics of their powerful alliance.

Gary was an undisputed superstar. Baker had been an All-Star and should have been entering his prime years, but alcohol addiction had hit him hard. After spending the lockout summer drinking and gaining weight, he was never the same player he had once been. Despite that, the Goodwins were able to leverage his history, his potential, and the possible wrath of Payton into a seven-year, maximum $86 million contract. It was a contract I begged the Club not to award him, based on his pitiful performance during the lockout season. But I was overruled. SuperSonics owners, the Ackerley family, were too afraid of the fallout from the Goodwins and Gary to take the stand that should have been taken. It was left to me and my staff to find a way through the woods.

There were plenty of enablers available to Vin. During one memorable meeting with me and SuperSonics President Wally Walker, one of our team leaders pleaded with them to stop taking Vin out drinking. "He has a serious problem that is bigger than basketball. It is ruining his life. Please, for his sake, as well as the good of our team, don't include him when you go out," we begged.

"No. He's twenty-seven years old, strong, and rich. He should be partying and enjoying himself," was the answer we received. Some teammate, huh?

This same key player also was forthcoming enough with me during another meeting I had with him to enlighten me in a way I will never forget. I asked him why he seemed to agree with the direction we were trying to take the team whenever we talked privately, only to be less-than-supportive about things in the press. His answer brought a tear to my eyes (and heart) on more than one level. "The people in the hood, at the barbershop, they want me to 'be the Man.' If I go along with you, I look like a slave to them."

That attitude reminded me of a conversation one of my players was overheard having with Philadelphia's Allen Iverson in the SuperSonic training room. It was several hours before a game, and Allen and the Seattle player both were there for treatments for respective minor ailments. Iverson was asked by another player how his relationship was going with his coach, Larry Brown. Everyone knew it had been rocky at times, but he answered that things were much improved. Upon hearing that, the SuperSonic shared some advice. "Don't let it get too smooth. You have to act up once in a while to show them who's 'the Man.'"

Gary Payton had a meltdown in Dallas during my last win as the Seattle coach, and it was directly related to my treatment of Vin Baker. Two games before our trip to play the Mavericks, we had lost to them in Seattle. During that game, I made a decision that brought me to the point of telling Wally Walker to fire me. I felt I deserved it (but I also wouldn't resign, because after all I'd endured, I deserved to get paid too) because I had chosen to play Baker for the sole reason of keeping the peace.

After signing Vin over my objections, I had tried my best to make things work. By starting him and giving him minutes, the hope was that he would either somehow regain his form, or we could trade him. But his play was so awful that both possibilities decreased as his game was exposed for the entire world to see.

"Wally, I knew we needed to go small to win. The key to beating one of Nellie's"—Don Nelson, Dallas Mavericks' coach—"teams has always been finding a way to match his quick lineups when he goes small, and retaining at least one position with a size/rebounding advantage they can't handle. In Phoenix, that guy used to be Tom Chambers, and later Barkley. The score might end up 146–140, but we would come out on top about 75 percent of the time. Anyway, when I put Vin on the bench in the third quarter, we put the perfect lineup out there to combat 'Nellieball.' We turned the game in our favor, but early in the fourth, I could tell by Vin's demeanor that he wasn't happy for the team's success. Neither was Payton. I caved and put him back in. Momentum swung back to Nellie, and we lost. Because of me."

Wally knew the history. He knew all about Baker's alcoholism. How Vin would hide "minis" of vodka in a toilet stall of the locker room so he could access them at halftime. Wally had supported me when Commissioner David Stern had tried to implement a new policy that would require all head coaches to wear a microphone during nationally televised games. Failure to do so would result in a $100,000 fine for both the coach and the organization.

Because of the necessity of monitoring Vin's soberness at all times, I tried to speak directly with the commissioner to explain to him my refusal to wear a mic, but he would neither speak with me nor budge. With the club's approval, I wrote Mr. Stern an "open letter" that outlined my position in such a way that put me on the side of truth, justice, and the American way. I acknowledged how interesting it might be for fans to get a peek into the inside of an NBA coach's locker room but made the case for the necessity of confidentiality regarding strategy and player relations. I pointed out how "interesting" it would be if Mr. Stern were "mic'd" during his planning sessions for any upcoming collective bargaining negotiations. Mike Lupica published it in his *New York Daily News* column, adding enough of his own spin to the controversy that the commissioner backed down!

But he didn't go quietly. He called Mike and delivered a low blow at me. "That was a nice letter you wrote for your boy, Mike."

"He wrote his own letter," Mike said, "and he was right, and you are wrong. You really should think these things through better before you issue edicts like this, David."

Wally also knew how I had tried to help Vin by putting him in touch with Pastor Ken Hutcherson. Hutch was the Pastor at Antioch Bible Church in the Seattle area. A former NFL linebacker, nobody messed with the self-nicknamed "Black Man." He loved to train Rottweilers and had a sign in his yard that read, "My Rottweiler can reach the fence in three seconds. Can you?"

If anyone could help Vin, Hutch would be the one. Baker's father was a Baptist pastor in Connecticut. He and his wife had raised Vin in a Christian home, and his NBA lifestyle had been concerning them for several years. In desperation, Rev. Baker had asked me to find help for his son and, with his approval, I recommended Hutch.

Hutch was raised in Alabama during a time of severe racial prejudice. His hatred was such that he started playing football so he could hurt White people legally. Then he met Jesus, and all that changed. After his NFL career was shortened by injury, he became the pastor of one of the most racially diverse churches in the world. His congregation looked like heaven will look, with every race of people included.

Vin had several "enablers" living at his house. They were always ready to party with him—at his expense, of course. The thought of putting them out of his life was inconceivable to him. He didn't want to appear to be "too good" for "friends" he'd known most of his life. Hutch had a solution for this. If Vin can't tell his "boys to get out, I plan on knocking on his door and announcing that my dogs will be entering the premises in fifteen minutes. They'll get out."

Baker's condition improved if he cooperated with Hutch. But he couldn't hang in there. When he slept through church one Sunday morning, he tried to lie his way out of facing the former linebacker with the truth. Too hungover to rise when Hutch's assistant pastor came to check on him, he directed the person who answered the door to say that he had gotten sick and was in the hospital.

We checked the hospitals, of course. When I called him out about his lie, I told him the same thing I would later tell DeMarcus Cousins. "I promised you that I would always tell you the truth to the best of my understanding. Even if the truth isn't pretty, I've kept my word. You owe Hutch, your teammates, and the organization an apology."

His response, instead, was that he had his people tell the media that "Westphal is trying to cram his religion down the players' throats." Stephen A. Smith was one member of the media who was happy to oblige on national TV.

With all that history to consider, Wally told me, "I'm not going to fire you now, and I don't want you to quit. Just promise me you won't make the same mistake again. Coach to win. Period."

Two games later, we were in Dallas. The game unfolded very much like it had when we had played them in Seattle a few days before. Only this time, I left Vin on the bench as we made a run late in the third quarter. As he fumed silently, Payton spoke up loudly. "We're too small. We need size. Put Vin in!"

"How about this," I answered. "You play, and I'll coach."

That was too much for him to take. He erupted with profanities and needed to be held back from jumping into my face by Assistant Coach Nate McMillan and others. I removed Gary from the game, but not from the bench. Whatever else one can say about Gary Payton, no one has ever said that he doesn't compete. After leaving him on the bench for the first few minutes of the final quarter, I reinserted him into the lineup. I let Vin keep sitting.

We won the game. I had coached the game to win, and I can remember very few more satisfying victories. There was fallout, of course. I decided to suspend Gary for his behavior. His reaction to the news was that of a broken person. I had never seen that side of him. Because I was so touched and convinced of his remorse, I foolishly chose to accept his apology and lift his suspension. I was convinced he had learned his lesson, and since he was working on a consecutive-games-played streak that was extremely important to him, I believed I could help smooth our relationship by allowing him to play. We got wiped out that night in San Antonio.

When we returned to Seattle for a Sunday afternoon practice, our morale was as low as it could get. I had attended church services at Antioch that morning. In the choir, right up front in the middle, was a man named Kenny. Kenny had a smile on his face as he sang and moved his head to the music. When people clapped, Kenny didn't. When they stood, Kenny stayed seated. But he sure kept smiling. He was a quadriplegic, so clapping and standing was impossible for him. But nobody smiled a more radiant smile than Kenny.

When practice began, I told the team about Kenny. "If Kenny can smile, why can't we? We get paid to play ball. We get paid a lot. We're healthy and get to play a game for a living. Let's stop feeling sorry for ourselves and make the most of what we have." I think most of the guys understood. I believed telling them about Kenny could build upon the foundation I had laid when I recounted the Tim Fultz story to them. We appeared to be on our way to the best practice of the year.

Except for Vin. He was not hustling. An emphasis of the practice was trying to improve our "talking on defense," but the only talking he did was to mutter various "f-bombs" referring to Kenny and directed at me. When I asked him to step off the floor if he wasn't going to give a real effort, he took things to another level. He left the gym and went straight to Wally Walker's office. When practice ended, I was the ex-coach of the Seattle SuperSonics.

I had seen the train wreck coming for quite a while. I thought back to when I had told the team the story of Tim Fultz and Southwestern College in the Denver visitor's locker room that snowy night. I was drained of emotion when the team took the floor after I finished speaking. My assistant coaches, Nate McMillan, Bob Weiss, and Dwane Casey, were putting on their neckties for the game.

"Do you think I made any dent at all on them? That was my best shot I just gave. I really hope some of them start to 'get it.'"

It was Bob Weiss who said, "I'm not sure if it penetrated any of *them*, but it sure spoke to Frank." He nodded in the direction of the most universally respected man in SuperSonics history, Head Athletic Trainer Frank Furtado. He was bawling to himself in a quiet corner of the room.

"It's time to tell the children
That it's not about the gold ...
But it is about the heart."

— John Stewart[10]

10 "The Man Who Would Be King (feat. Yes)." Musixmatch: The World's Largest Lyrics Catalog. Accessed June 26, 2024. https://www.musixmatch.com/lyrics/John-Stewart-feat-Yes-2/The-Man-Who-Would-Be-King-feat-Yes.

EPILOGUE

Arizona Christian University kept growing. The school had been busting out of the twenty-acre campus that had once seemed massive. When it was Southwestern College with only 200 students and three buildings, it probably was. But under President Len Munsil's leadership and an unwavering commitment to remaining true to the Scriptures and a conservative biblical worldview, ACU had been quietly becoming one of the most respected Christian schools in the country. But without room to grow, it seemed they would never be able to take the steps necessary to offer the campus experience students would expect from such a school.

I believe it was truly miraculous that the Tim Fultz Memorial Gymnasium ever came into being. I don't believe Southwestern College could have survived and become Arizona Christian University without it. I don't know why I would believe that God was out of miracles, but I pretty much thought it would be ACU's destiny to remain on the comparatively tiny, now land-locked piece of desert until Jesus returns. But then Arizona State University offered to trade a highly developed sixty-eight-acre jewel of a campus that had housed the Thunderbird School of Global Management in exchange for ACU's more strategically located twenty acres. The ACU Board of Trustees agreed that God's hand had to be all over the trade. As a member of the ACU Board of Trustees, I was honored to vote in favor of this miraculous transaction. We felt that for ACU to be able to properly have a chance to fulfill its goal to "Transform Culture with Truth," the school would have to grow. And this amazing campus upgrade was more than an answer to prayer, since we had never even dreamed to ask for such an impossible upgrade.

"Transform Culture with Truth." That's an ambitious goal. "Truth" can be a loaded word. In the Book of Jeremiah, the Lord says, "and you will seek Me and find Me when you search for Me with all your heart." Then, Jesus Himself said, "I am the Way, the Truth, and the Life, no one comes to the Father except through Me," as well as "Seek ye first the Kingdom of God." When these instructions are coupled with His admonition "My Kingdom is not of this world," it becomes apparent that the "Truth" being talked about in the Bible is of an eternal nature. The goal of "transforming culture," even when it means involving oneself in politics, can never mean compromising Truth.

We are all just passing through this world. None of us can know the heart of another, hence God's admonition that we should not judge another's heart. Nor can we completely explain God's ways.

Mark Twain told of a foolish man who claimed to be able to do just that. So he was challenged to explain the fate of a man who was simply out walking his dog, only to have a safe fall on his head and kill him. "Why did God allow the safe to fall on that man and crush him? Why not just have it fall on the animal and spare the man?"

The question did cause the fool to hesitate, but then he figured it out. "It's obvious. The dog woulda seen it coming!"

"Create in me a clean heart, O God, and renew a steadfast spirit in me …" (Psalm 51:10). As long as we have breath, it is never too late to die to self and to trust in the Lord who has a plan for our lives. Surrendering to Him removes the blinders from our eyes so we can realize His ways are higher than our ways. And that His love letter to us Genesis to Revelation is infallible, containing all we need to know about who He is, who we are without Him, and who we are with Him. Do we want to be like the dog who can see what's coming? Or do we want to remain oblivious to His warnings to come? It's our choice. No one will have an excuse.

Wayward athletes in basketball or any sport, dysfunctional families, corrupt governments on down the line … when hearts change, so will the culture. A culture of God's righteousness. That's the truth that Tim Fultz died believing, even as he was living it out. That's the truth Arizona Christian University is dedicated to spreading.

"Let us not talk falsely now, the hour is getting late."

— Bob Dylan[1]

---

1 "All Along the Watchtower | The Official Bob Dylan Site." The Official Bob Dylan Site. Accessed June 21, 2024. https://www.bobdylan.com/songs/all-along-watchtower/.

IN LOVING MEMORY OF TIM FULTZ

Arizona Christian University created a tribute to Tim Fultz that was displayed in the lobby outside the gymnasium that bore his name on the former campus of Southwestern College.

That large plaque and photograph are now displayed outside the gymnasium at the Firestorm Recreation Center, near a tribute to Paul Westphal, on the University's new campus in Glendale.

The memorial reads:

"Tim Fultz
1966–1990
Student, Athlete, Missionary.

As a student, Tim spent his academic life at Southwestern College preparing to be a missionary. It was his one desire to serve the Lord on the mission field.

As an athlete, Paul Westphal called him one of the MVPs of the 1985–86 basketball season, not because of his athletic skills, but because he had a car in which to transport the real players to a practice gym several miles away from the college. But with just a few seconds left in a game that would propel those young fledgling Eagles into the playoffs, Tim became the hero by hitting two crucial free throws to win the game by three points, and helped the team qualify for the 1986 National Little College Athletic Association Tournament.

While serving as a missionary in Africa, Tim fell thirty-five feet to his death on August 3rd, 1990. His heart was always bent on being a missionary to Africa and went on several trips to build churches and share the message of Jesus Christ. Today his heart still beats in Africa after giving his heart and several vital organs to Africans after his death.

THE SERVANT

He was not the most skillful or the best
But he had worked hard
Under the watchful eye of his coach
Under the watchful eye of his God
Learning, practicing, training, waiting
To play
To serve
The basketball game hung in the balance
The souls of many hung in the balance
Building upon a winning record
Building a house of worship
And when the final shot fell
And when he fell
They carried him off, cheering
They carried him off
He had played with heart
He gave his heart
They called him a hero
The Lord called him home
O, death, where is thy sting?
O, grave, where is thy victory?
The sting of death is sin; and
The strength of sin is the law.
But thanks be to God,
Who giveth us the victory
Through our Lord
Jesus Christ.

Therefore, my beloved brethren, be ye steadfast, unmovable,
Always abounding in the work of the Lord,
Forasmuch as ye know that your labor is not in vain in the Lord.
- 1 Corinthians 15:55-58

Well done, good and faithful servant.
In Loving Memory of Tim Fultz"

A NOTE FROM CINDY WESTPHAL

I woke up at two or three in the morning. It was dark in the room, but there was no Paul … so quiet you could hear a pin drop. His playing days had been over for a while. In fact, he was in between coaching jobs, so it seemed rest should come more easily now. I got up to wander from one dark room to the next, finding him alone at his desk … the only light source being that from his computer shining on his face. He was typing away. Whatever it was about, he was in a zone … so I knew not to disturb him till he came up for air.

Paul explained he had been jotting down notes to himself over the years. Things that made him laugh during his basketball career, things that challenged and stretched his thinking, and strengthened his faith. He loved the creativity of basketball more than strict X's and O's. He was quoted once in *Sports Illustrated* as saying, basketball is "like a chess game with soul." As both a player and a coach there, of course, always needed to be a game plan, but never at the expense of creativity for those players who had that special mind and skillset to pull it off. Not to Paul's way of thinking, anyway. He also was making notes about the diverse individuals he was blessed to meet and know and call friends along the way.

Paul said he thought he might write a book someday. He had witnessed the League and the game itself change so much since the day he was drafted by the Boston Celtics in '72. Team camaraderie was disappearing, replaced by friends who'd travel on their own to road games to hang out instead of players building relationships with their teammates. Plays seemed more "canned" and less creative. Slower. Even boring.

Paul was the consummate gamesman. If a game wasn't fun, he didn't see any reason to play. Though he enjoyed many fun seasons as a player and a coach, one stands out as especially fun because of its innocence and everyone's respect for one another. The other stands out like, as he often would put it, going to the dentist for a root canal every day. Not fun at all.

Paul's hindsight comparison between these two teams kept racing in his mind. He sat weeks on end at his computer for hours till he'd put it on the shelf for a few months, before returning to it refreshed, another chapter in the works. Then again, he'd put it aside for maybe a year till there were more chapters to add. And so, it went for a few decades.

Paul finished writing less than a year before he was diagnosed with glioblastoma, his dream of having his book published never realized. After he passed, our daughter, Tori, and I found the manuscript exactly where he left it … "on the shelf." It became our passion to see it through in his honor. We laughed and we cried as we could hear his voice while reading aloud to one another. We hope, dear reader, that you have too.

A NOTE FROM TORI WESTPHAL HIGA

It was the morning of our son, Kai's, sixth grade graduation ceremony in July of 2020. We were preparing for the big day when I got a call that would forever change our lives. My parents called to say that they were on their way to two different hospitals, my mom for an emergency appendectomy, and my dad to get a brain MRI.

They told me not to come because I'd miss Kai's graduation—that they'd be fine. When I told my husband the situation, he told me that I had to go to be with them. He said they had been there for me in every aspect of my life and now it was my turn.

My head spun with all that was going on. I packed my bag for the hotel that was an hour away with three or four pairs of pajamas and not enough normal clothes to wear by day because I could barely think straight. When I arrived at the hospital to see my dad, it was amid COVID-19 protocols and we both had to wear N-95 masks for the visit. His room was large and cold, and his brain scan was on display in the center of it. My heart broke into a million pieces when I could see the large masses in both the center and the right side of his brain. We weren't given the official diagnosis at this point, but a picture was all we needed to see to know how serious it was.

I'll never forget what he told me through his mask as he gestured toward the scan. He said, "I'm worried that this is going to be the worst-case scenario. But I'm not afraid of dying … because I know where I'm going (Heaven). The hardest part will be saying goodbye to everyone."

Through my tears at that moment and for all the tears that came during and after his six-month brain cancer journey that would end up taking his life, those words were the best thing I could have possibly heard. They brought and continue to bring so much comfort to my soul. He knew where he was going.

This book is mostly about where he has been. He spent twenty-five years on and off again working on this book. I have had the great pleasure of reading several different versions of his manuscript over the years, each one better than the last. He completed his final manuscript a few months before his cancer diagnosis, and I am so grateful to have his words in print.

I believe everyone has at least one book inside of them—and this is my dad's book, his story. It has a basketball backdrop, but it's about so much more than just basketball. It's about life. It's about where he's been and, if you look closely enough, it's about how he could know where he was going too.

ACKNOWLEDGMENTS
BY CINDY WESTPHAL AND TORI WESTPHAL HIGA

Westy has always been a part of a team, so it makes sense that this book would be a team effort. The group of people who came together to make it possible are forever in our deepest gratitude.

As his wife and daughter, we have had the honor of doing the first edits of this book. But we knew we couldn't have done it without the help we were so blessed to receive.

First, we'd like to express our heartfelt thanks to Dr. Tracy Munsil and President Len Munsil of Arizona Christian University. They were the first to catch the vision for this book and have been an inspiration, encouragement, and wealth of knowledge as the publishers through Arizona Christian University Press ever since. They have been there for us from the very beginning, making things happen all along the way. Thank you both!

We'd also like to thank the entire Arizona Christian University Board of Trustees, especially Andrew Unkefer, Don King, Wayne Mihailov, and Rick Blankenship, without whose personal generosity this book literally would not have made it "off the shelf." Paul was honored to be an ACU Trustee with you. He famously hated meetings, but the fact that he sat through so many while serving for six years as an ACU Trustee is testimony to how much he loved ACU and enjoyed being with all of you who served with him. We are so grateful and thank you from the bottom of our hearts for all you meant to him.

We couldn't be more thankful for our endorsers. Not just endorsers, but also for their friendship in life. We greatly appreciate the time they took to read this book and know Paul would have been beyond humbled by your kind words.

Thank you to Brenda and Kim Cates, and Zach Cates, as our faithful longtime friends for always being there for us … whether it was moving in with us to help as caregivers for Paul fighting glioblastoma or always being available to bounce things off of in life, and with this book since his passing … providing wisdom and refreshing memories. You could hear his voice along with us. It's meant so much. We love you more than words can say!

We'd like to thank Victoria Duerstock and her incredibly talented team at End Game Press. Her expertise, kind and encouraging demeanor, and her vision and drive took Westy's book to the next level. And it didn't hurt that she loves basketball, too! We know that Paul's book turned out to be the best version of itself directly because of Victoria's leadership.

Most of all, we thank our Savior and Lord Jesus Christ. Because it was Paul's heart, it was ours as well that God would be glorified within these pages, for His faithfulness to see him through the ups and downs of his career. And life. The good decisions, and poor decisions. Even foolish ones, being that we're all human. That our Creator has a sense of humor, too. That He promises to "never leave or forsake" (Hebrews 13:5, ESV) those who put their trust in Him for salvation.

This book was a labor of love, and we are beyond thankful for the team of people that we believe God put together to see it come to fruition. Thank you to everyone listed here, and to all those who have been in Paul's and our lives as trusted friends. Our gratitude runs deep.